DISTINGUISHING MORAL EDUCATION,
VALUES CLARIFICATION AND RELIGION-STUDIES

AMERICAN ACADEMY OF RELIGION
SECTION PAPERS

edited by
John Priest

Number 18

DISTINGUISHING   MORAL   EDUCATION,
VALUES CLARIFICATION AND RELIGION-STUDIES

Religion-Studies in Public Education
1976 Proceedings
edited by
Nicholas Piediscalzi and Barbara Ann Swyhart

SCHOLARS PRESS
Missoula, Montana

DISTINGUISHING MORAL EDUCATION, VALUES   CLARIFICATION AND RELIGION-STUDIES

RELIGION-STUDIES IN PUBLIC EDUCATION: 1976 PROCEEDINGS

edited by

Nicholas Piediscalzi

and

Barbara Ann Swyhart

Published by

SCHOLARS PRESS

for

AMERICAN ACADEMY OF RELIGION

Distributed by

SCHOLARS PRESS
University of Montana
Missoula, Montana 59801

DISTINGUISHING MORAL EDUCATION, VALUES CLARIFICATION AND RELIGION-STUDIES

edited by

Nicholas Piediscalzi

and

Barbara Ann Swyhart

Library of Congress Cataloging in Publication Data
American Academy of Religion. Religion-Studies in
   Public Education Group.
   Distinguishing moral education, values, clarification,
and religion-studies.

   Papers for the 1976 annual meeting of the American
Academy of Religion.
   Bibliography: p.
   1. Moral education—Congresses. I. Piediscalzi,
Nicholas. II. Swyhart, Barbara Ann DeMartino.
III. American Academy of Religion.IV. Title.
LC268.A53 1976   370.11'4   76-26670
ISBN 0-89130-082-1

Printed in the United States of America

Printing Department
University of Montana
Missoula, Montana 59801

TABLE OF CONTENTS

PREFACE

Nicholas Piediscalzi

Wright State University
Dayton, Ohio 45431

A BRIEF HISTORY OF THE GROUP

Religion-Studies in Public Education became an
official concern of the American Academy of Religion
(AAR) in 1973 when the officers of the organization in-
vited this author to convene a consultation on the topic
at the 1974 Annual Meeting. Those who attended the consultation heard a panel describe recent developments and
problems in this emerging new area. Ways in which the
AAR could take cognizance of and serve its needs also
were suggested.[1] The consultation members voted unani-
mously to request the AAR Program Committee to establish
a Group on Public Schools Religion-Studies whose major
concerns would be theoretical issues and practical
problems.

The Program Committee acted positively on the
request. Nicholas Piediscalzi and Barbara Ann Swyhart
were appointed co-chairpersons. They along with Guntram
Bischoff constituted a steering committee. The Group met
for the first time at the 1975 Annual Meeting. Three
different problems were discussed: (1) "Blueprints for
the Future? Michigan's Certification Programs in the
Academic Study of Religions" by Paul J. Will; (2) "Religion in Human Culture: The Development of a Model Course
in World Religions" by Lee Smith and Wes Bodin; and (3)
"Pedagogical and Normative Issues in Public Education
Religion-Studies." Under this heading, three separate
papers were presented: "Public Education Religion-Studies: Toward An Operational Process Methodology for
Science, Religion and Ethics" by Barbara Ann Swyhart;
"The Problem of Norm in Public Education Religion-Stud-
ies: Enlightenment, Emancipation or Socialization" by
John Whitney; and "The Pedagogy of Religiology," by
Guntram G. Bischoff.[2]

The steering committee, including two new members,
Paul J. Will and Robert Hall, met in January of 1976 to
consider evaluations of the 1975 sessions and to make
longrange plans. Three major actions were taken. First,
The Group's title was changed to Religion-Studies in
Public Education. This was done to clarify the academic
purpose and emphases of the Group and to prevent erroneous identification of it with the Public Education Religion Studies Center (PERSC). Second, the committee
agreed to co-sponsor with PERSC a Consultation on
"Initiating Religion-Studies in Public Education,"
October 27-28, 1976 in St. Louis, Missouri, just prior to
the opening of the AAR Annual Meeting. Third, the
committee decided that the Group's major goal should be
the preparation of policy statements and/or guidelines

over a four year period on major issues in religion-studies in public education. The issues are: (1) Distinguishing Moral Education, Values Clarification and
Religion-Studies (1976); (2) Religion-Studies as A
Distinct Discipline in Public Education (1977); (3) Professional Programs for Religion-Studies in Public Education (1978); and (4) Paradigms for Religion-Studies in
Public Education (1979).

The committee members singled out these areas
because they believe that religion-studies in public
education is an academic field in its own right with its
own pedagogy. Also, it is important and necessary to
distinguish it from the disciplines and fields with which
it frequently is confused. Furthermore, the committee
contends that it is imperative to deliniate and describe
carefully and succinctly the unique academic characteristics of religion-studies in public education and the
philosophical and academic rationales, norms and goals
for college and university research and education programs in this area.

1976 Program Theme

DISTINGUISHING MORAL EDUCATION, VALUES CLARIFICATION
AND RELIGION-STUDIES

In recent years moral education and values clarification courses or units have been introduced into the
curricula of public schools. At least four reasons for
their appearance can be isolated. First, some scholars
and teachers realize that any form of study or education
involves moral and value questions. To ignore or omit
such issues is to misrepresent the educational process.
Guntram Bischoff, for example, states that any theory of
public education is not complete without the formulation
of objectives and goals. "If this is granted," Bischoff
continues, "it follows automatically that values must be
considered since goals in fact imply and constitute
values. The very question of the academic legitimation
of religion-studies in the public school necessarily implies the value question. And this is true even if one
would adopt the. . . positivist stance since socialization (respect for law, pluralism, tolerance and understanding, etc.) is an inalienable concern of public
school pedagogy."[3]

A second reason for the introduction of moral education and values clarification is found among those who
hold that the purpose of education is not to provide
students with doctrainaire answers but rather introduce
them to a process of inquiry whereby they are enabled to
develop their own reasoned conclusions about life's most
important questions and adopt their own moral positions.
Since human beings, according to this group, are creators
of meanings and values, students must be introduced
to the principles and processes by which these meanings
and values are fashioned so that they will be able both
(1) to understand themselves and others more accurately;

and (2) establish their own meanings and values with more precision and self-awareness.

A third group desires to introduce moral education and values clarification because its proponents believe that both our pluralistic nation and emerging world community require such study in order to prepare students to deal effectively with the plurality and diversity of moral positions and values systems which confront them.

The changes in our socio-economic life and the problems confronting our nation move a fourth group to call for the introduction of moral education and values clarification--in the doctrainaire sense--to solve our nation's problems. Since this group receives very little direct attention in the following papers and since it is the one most responsible for the erroneous identification of moral education, values clarification and religion-studies, I shall comment on it in detail.

The activities of this group need to be seen as an extension of efforts in the 1950's to re-introduce "spiritual" values into our society. The dramatic changes in and problems confronted by post-World War II America were attributed to a loss of "spiritual" values. America would get back to normal and solve its problems, it was assumed, by returning to the "old virtues" of the Republic. Very few people were certain what they were and most people--including national leaders--did not bother to find out. No less a figure than President Eisenhower called for a return to faith and added that it did not matter what faith just so as long as it was faith. However, behind this call for undifferentiated "spiritual" values and faith is, I believe, a desire to return to Cotton Mather's basic virtues: "If you will remember four words and attempt all that is comprised in them, OBEDIENCE, HONESTY, INDUSTRY, AND PIETY, you will be the blessings and the Josephs of the families to which you belong."[4] Of course, Mather's Calvinistic theology is no longer included as the foundation of these virtues. Also, the structures of our society neither foster nor sanction these virtues.

W. B. Lauderdale, in an insightful essay, points out that American education has passed through four major stages. Each, except the last, has had a moral intention. During the Colonial Period the purpose of the school system was "eternal salvation and the preservation of the state."[5] This is the time when the moral intent of the educational system was undergirded thoroughly by Calvinistic theology. Lauderdale also adds that the morality of the schools during this time sought to meet the needs of the children of those in positions of power "as future state and religious leaders and serve the state through [inculcating] the obedience of the [children of] the poor."[6]

The second stage began to emerge during the mid-eighteenth century and lasted until the mid-nineteenth. This is a period of transition. "A shift from a purely religious to a political and prudential orientation occurred."[7] As a result, the moral intent of the schools became associated with patriotism and good citizenship. Calvinist theology remained the foundation of this morality but the Enlightenment diminished its emotional fervor.

The appearance of the common school in the mid-nineteenth century marks the beginning of the third stage. To serve the needs of an industrializing and expanding America the schools introduced "a massive training program for teaching skills required by industry."[8] Concommitantly, the religious and moral intent of the schools changed. Horace Mann introduced non-sectarian religious education as a way to avoid the divisiveness of sectarianism and moral teaching became "direct political teaching, a move inspired by the transition from a theocracy to a democracy."[9] Morality became "political morality as a function of citizenship."[10]

The fourth and present stage of American education is an extension of the third. The schools remain vocationally oriented, only more so. "Labor needs are now the most important criteria for giving direction to the development of school programs. Theistic and humanistic "moral intentions have, for a long time, been relegated a minor role in the face of such marketplace requirements."[11] But the values of the marketplace do not unite us as a people. They tear us apart. We began to address this problem, as noted earlier, by calling for the re-introduction of "spiritual" values and faith. Also, in the interim, "the national dialogue has shifted from moral and religious concerns to the concern that the schools not be labeled 'Godless'.... It seems that the current intent by many is to keep the public schools from being irreligious, and a token reference to a diety at a convenient hour will suffice."[12]

Lauderdale asserts that these most recent developments reveal that "there exists [today] no moral intent--nothing to offer which would be unique to a democratic people--merely a survival technique for existing institutions."[13] This being the case, neither the introduction of moral education, values clarification and or religion-studies nor the erroneous identification of these fields will provide a new moral intent for our schools and nation. Therefore, it is important to keep this in mind as we formulate our guidelines. We need to show that the recent introduction of moral education, values clarification and religion-studies usually becomes in the public forum an extension of the call of the 1950's for undifferentiated "spiritual" values and faith and that both are part of a stage of development in American education which is without moral intent, in Lauderdale's sense of the term. Also, we need to emphasize that religious and moral reformations come not from providing young people with new techniques but from adults consciously and actively choosing to transform their religious, moral and political institutions. Hence it is erroneous and counter-productive to expect our schools to solve the religious and moral problems of our day solely by introducing the techniques of moral education, values clarification and/or religion-studies.[14]

Furthermore, it must be made clear that public schools in a pluralistic democracy cannot foster one faith or one set of values for the purpose of reuniting our nation. The difficult task of providing an overarching worldview for our pluralistic society must be assumed by the larger community. It is a complex and difficult one which does not lend itself to an easy or quick solution.

Finally, we need to recognize that present discussions on moral education and values education usually do not pay sufficient attention to the fact that moral positions and the worldviews from which they are derived are not totally dependent upon rational principles or clarification techniques. Rather, they are based upon faith commitments which are made at the unconscious level where feelings, symbols, stories and rituals are significant determinative factors.[15] In this context, we also need to point out that many of the theories and methods of moral education and values clarification now in vogue are established on covert and unexamined faith commitments and values systems. Moreover, these presentations usually center on individual decision making and ignore the significant way in which moral decisions are communal decisions. Therefore, one of the reasons for distinguishing among moral education, values clarification and religion-studies is to point out the significant role societal religious--theistic and secular--commitments play in moral formation and values systems.

In raising these issues I do not intend to reject outright moral education or values clarification. They have a place in the curriculum. I only want to point out that many people erroneously identify these activities with religion-studies, and hold unrealistic expectations for them. Also, I want to call attention to the fact that moral education and values clarification as now practiced usually present only the rational and individual dimensions of morals and values and frequently covertly put forth a faith commitment. Our guidelines must be written with these problems in mind.

In conclusion, besides making clear and succinct distinctions between moral education, values clarification and religion-studies, it will be necessary for us to show, as do the authors of the following papers, that the introduction of these fields into the schools must be justified on solid educational grounds. As a resource for this final task, I include below two statements from PERSC's Guidebook, Public Education Religion-Studies: Questions and Answers,[16] which suggest an educational justification and goals for public education religion-studies. The first was prepared by the PERSC staff and the second by the Florida State University Religion-Social Studies Curriculum Project. (They are presented here with the permission of both groups who hold copyright to them.)

6.

A Rationale for Religion-Studies in Public Education

The religious factor in human history is a significant one. It is deeply embedded in most of the world's history, in its literary documents, and in its social institutions. Consequently a curriculum which does not include study about religion is incomplete. As Raymond English, Director of the Educational Research Council of America's Social Science Program, points out, students are deprived of knowledge of an important dimension of human experience:

> To study human behavior and societies without paying attention to religious motivations is like studying chemistry without recognizing the presence of oxygen in the atmosphere. Men behave as they do for a variety of reasons, and one powerful causal factor is their value system--their beliefs about life's meaning and purpose. these beliefs are their religion-- their ultimate concept of reality.

Moreover, to exclude religion studies from the school is, as the American Association of School Administrators suggested in 1964, to misrepresent religion and to distort history:

> A curriculum which ignored religion would itself have serious religious implications. It would seem to proclaim that religion has not been as real in men's lives as health or politics or economics. By omission it would appear to deny that religion has been and is important in man's history--a denial of the obvious. In day-by-day practice, the topic cannot be avoided. As an integral part of man's culture, it must be included.

Thus, since one of the public schools' tasks is to provide students with a complete education, study about religion must be made a part of the curriculum.

Also, in a time like ours when societal values are changing and world cultural values come into conflict, it is important to study about the sources of values. Religion is a source of values for many societies and peoples. Therefore, it is important for the public schools to help students understand the role of religion in value formation and value conservation or transformation.

In summary, commitment to comprehensive education requires the inclusion of religion studies in the curriculum.[17]

Suggested General Goals for Public
Education Religion-Studies

The Florida State University Religion-Social
Studies Curriculum Project staff suggests that the general
goals for public education religion studies should
include:

I. An understanding of

    A. The nature of religion
       1. Its essential characteristics
       2. Its development, organization, and
          transmission
       3. Its universality and variety

    B. The place (or role) of religion
       1. Religion in its cultural context
       2. Its relation to economic, social,
          political, educational, and domestic
          institutions
       3. Its relation to man's humanistic
          endeavors: art, music, language,
          literature, etc.

    C. The methods of study in religion
       1. The variety of ways of inquiry
       2. The legitimacy of the study of
          religion, and the distinction between
          study of and adherence to religion

II. An appreciation of

    A. The place of religion in human history

    B. The role of religion in private motiva-
       tions, habits, and aspirations

    C. The varieties of religious expressions,
       understandings, and effects

    D. The necessity for mutual tolerance

III. Development of skills in

    A. Perceptive application of the processes of
       inquiry to religious concepts

    B. Intelligent development of moral reasoning
       and value judgment

    C. Careful description of religious phenomena

    D. Fair-minded explanations of religious
       practices and beliefs[18]

The 1976 Working Papers

The following papers serve as theoretical and
practical resources for the Group's members as they begin
formulating a set of guidelines for clarifying the
differences among moral education, values clarification
and religion-studies. Robert Hall's paper describes the
major differences and interrelations between moral education and religion-studies. Barbara Swyhart summarizes
and evaluates the major movements in contemporary moral
education and values clarification and their relationships to religion-studies in public education. She also
provides a selected bibliography. John Meyer's article
presents helpful background information from his working
experiences in Canada and his study of developments in
Great Britain and the United States. His paper is
included at the request of Barbara Ann Swyhart who
believes it provides concrete information which will help
us understand more thoroughly values education and clarification as we try to distinguish between them and
religion-studies.

Notes

[1]Panel members were: Guntram Bischoff, Joseph Forcinelli, Edwin Gaustad, John Meyer, Robert Michaelsen, Nicholas Piediscalzi, Barbara Ann Swyhart and John Whitney.

[2]These papers were published by the American Academy of Religion and Scholars Press in 1975, Anne Carr and Nicholas Piediscalzi, Editors, The Academic Study of Religion: 1975/Public Schools Religion-Studies: 1975 (Preprinted Papers for the Academic Study of Religion Section and the Public Schools Religion-Studies Group).

[3]May 13, 1976 letter from Guntram Bischoff to Nicholas Piediscalzi.

[4]Cotton Mather, Bonifacius: An Essay upon the Good. Edited with an introduction by David Levin. Cambridge, Massachusetts: The Belknap Press of Harvard University Press, 1966, p. 56.

[5]William B. Lauderdale, "Moral Intentions in the History of American Education," Theory Into Practice, Vol. XIV, No. 4 (October, 1975), p. 265.

[6]Ibid.

[7]Ibid., p. 266.

[8]Ibid., p. 269.

[9]Ibid., p. 268.

[10]Ibid.

[11]Ibid., p. 269.

[12]Ibid., p. 267.

[13]Ibid., p. 270.

[14]Vitezslav Gardavsky, God Is Not Yet Dead, Harmondsworth, Middlesex, England: Penguin Books Ltd, 1973, pp. 26-27 and 50-51 asserts that the Greek view of reality which gave rise to the Western "scientific" attitude is based on a closed mechanical model which fosters a confident belief in the capacity of human beings to master all forces in reality through the development of skills and techniques. This view, according to him, is inadequate because it does not take human history into account. It is keyed to a dead past and closed system rather than to the future and new options. He contrasts this view with that of the Hebrews where emphasis is placed upon history, the future and man's opportunity to create new meanings and structures through active choice as historical needs change. This contrast

Notes, Page Two

helps us isolate the types of worldviews now informing
our educational philosophies and our approaches to moral
education, values clarification and religion-studies.
Also, I would identify many of the "popular" approaches
to moral education and value clarification as "Greek" and
inadequate for our historical needs since they emphasize
technique rather than active choice.

[15]Cf. Peter Gedge, "Morals and Religion" in Ninian
Smart and Donald Horder, (eds), New Movements in Religious
Education. London: Temple Smith, 1975, p. 57. "ME
[Moral Education] which confines itself to rationalist
assumptions or fails to ask basic questions of meaning,
purpose and value is inadequate. Such questions are
common to ME and RE, [Religious Education] so a proper ME
will include not merely the skills of moral decision-
making but also content, and a fair survey of the range
of answers to its questions will include answers given
by at least two or three alternative traditions,
religious and non-religious."

[16]Dayton Ohio: Public Education Religion Studies
Center, 1974.

[17]Ibid., p. 3.

[18]Ibid., p. 4.

SELECTED BIBLIOGRAPHY

Theoretical and Legal Issues

Boles, Donald E. THE BIBLE, RELIGION, AND THE PUBLIC SCHOOLS. Iowa State University Press. 1965.

_____. THE TWO SWORDS: COMMENTARIES AND CASES IN RELIGION. Iowa State University Press. 1967.

Duker, Sam. THE PUBLIC SCHOOLS AND RELIGION: THE LEGAL CONTEXT. Harper and Row. 1966.

Engle, David E.,(ed.). RELIGION IN PUBLIC EDUCATION. Paulist Press. 1973.

Fellman, David, (ed.). THE SUPREME COURT AND EDUCATION. Columbia University Press. 1962.

Holm, Jean L. TEACHING RELIGION IN SCHOOL. Oxford University Press. 1975.

Kauper, Paul G. RELIGION AND THE CONSTITUTION. Louisiana State University Press. 1964.

Michaelsen, Robert. PIETY IN THE PUBLIC SCHOOL. Macmillan. 1970.

Sizer, Theodore R., (ed.) RELIGION AND PUBLIC EDUCATION. Houghton Mifflin. 1967.

Curriculum Materials

THE BIBLE READER: AN INTERFAITH INTERPRETATION (Benziger, Bruce, and Glencoe).

RELIGIOUS LITERATURE OF THE WEST (Augsburg Publishing House).

GANDHI, BUDDHISM, CONFUCIANISM, AND TAOISM (Addison-Wesley Pub. Co.).

THE BIBLE AS/IN LITERATURE (Scott, Foresman, and Co.).

RELIGIOUS-PHILOSOPHICAL SYSTEMS (Rand McNally and Co.).

GOD AND GOVERNMENT (Addison-Wesley Publishing Co.).

GOD-AND-MAN NARRATIVE: THE RELIGIOUS STORY (University of Nebraska Press).

FOUR WORLD VIEWS (Allyn and Bacon). Boston, Massachusetts 02210.

ISSUES IN RELIGION (Addison-Wesley Publishing Company).

12.
AUDIO-VISUAL RESOURCES

Teaching: A Question of Method is a six-minute, 16mm
color film in the series "Citizenship: Whose Responsibility?" released by International Film Bureau, 332 South
Michigan Ave., Chicago, Illinois 60604. The purchase
price is $75.00; the rental fee is $10.00. This film is
concerned with the question of the degree to which a high
school teacher has the right to deliberately attempt to
alter or change beliefs which are common to contemporary
American culture. Among such beliefs are those in the
sanctity of capitalism, democracy, the home, and the
Judaic-Christian body of ethical and religious teachings.

Religion in Public Schools was originally an NBC-TV
broadcast in the FRONTIERS OF FAITH series. The film
features Dr. Philip Phenix, professor of philosophy and
education at Teachers College, Columbia University, who
is interviewed by Henry J. McCorkle, editor of THE
EPISCOPALIAN magazine. The interview begins with a discussion of the implications of the 1963 Supreme Court
decision on Bible reading in the public schools and moves
on to examples of religious issues in literature,
history, and even mathematics. This is a 29-minute,
black-and-white 16 mm film produced by the National
Broadcasting Company and now available through the
Broadcasting and Film Commission, 475 Riverside Drive,
New York, New York 10029. The rental fee is $10.00.

Keystone for Education. An award-winning documentary
film designed to answer the many questions on religion
and the public schools. Includes an analysis of the
court decisions by leading experts and an explanation of
curricular activities by classroom teachers. A 28-
minute, 16 mm color print. $20.00 rental. $265.00 purchase. A study guide available for $3.25 includes the
complete text of the film and supplemental material.
(Educational Communication Association, 960 National
Press Building, Washington, D.C. 20004).

The Schempp Case. A documentary film that presents the
issues of the Schempp decision in dramatic fashion. Included is a re-creation of the emotionally charged issues
as presented to the court and an analysis of the guidelines established by the court. (Encyclopedia Britan-
nica Educational Corporation, 425 North Michigan Avenue,
Chicago, Ill. 60611).

Learning About Religion. A series of four films by the
Religion-Social Studies Curriculum Project (Florida State
University, Tallahassee, Florida 32306). The First film,
"The Supreme Court Speaks: Learning About Religion in
the Public Schools," is a general one dealing with the
overall possibilities for the study of religion in public
schools, including legal questions. The other three
films are similar in format to each other and each one
emphasizes a different subject. The first deals with the

study of religion in American culture or history courses
("Learning About Religion in American History Courses");
the second with the study of religion in world cultures
or world history courses ("Learning About Religion in
World Culture Courses"); and the third with the study of
religion in social issues courses, such as civics, problems of democracy. etc. ("Learning About Religion in
Social Issues Courses"). The effective use of these
films would involve the first film and only one of the
last three films. It would be repetitious to show all
three of the last films. These films are available from
the following sources:

Media Center   Audio-Visual Center
University of Minnesota   Indiana University
Minneapolis, Minnesota 55455   Bloomington, Indiana 47401

Public Education Religion Studies Center
Wright State University
Dayton, Ohio 45431

Media Center   Media Center
Florida State University   University of California
Tallahassee, Florida 32306   Berkeley, California 94720

Organizations to Write for Assistance

Florida State University Religion-Social Studies
Curriculum Project, 426 Hull Drive, Florida State
University, Tallahassee, Florida 32306.

Indiana University Institute on Teaching the Bible in
Secondary English, Sycamore Hall 201, Bloomington,
Indiana 47401.

National Council on Religion and Public Education, Ball
State University, Muncie, Indiana 47306.

Public Education Religion Studies Center, Wright State
University, Dayton, Ohio 45431.

World Religions Curriculum Development Center, 6425 West
33rd Street, Minneapolis, Minnesota 55426.

MORAL EDUCATION AND RELIGION STUDIES
Robert T. Hall
The College of Steubenville

It is not surprising that the two fields of moral education and religion studies are very much confused in the popular mind. For most people morality means religion and religion is largely a matter of moral teachings. This opinion is common among both educators and clergy; it is even more common than it perhaps ought to be among professors of religion.

The position I shall take is that this view is quite misguided, that religion studies and moral education are two very distinct disciplines, that they ought to be treated separately for academic purposes, and that the confusion of the two inhibits educators from developing a clear idea of the principles and purposes of education in either field. Only when these two fields are kept separate, I shall say, can we expect to be able to develop programs in each field which will be adequate to the needs of public education. Before I present my reasons for this conviction, however, there is one preliminary consideration which seems to me quite important.

THE PRINCIPLE OF NON-INDOCTRINATION

The basic principle which I take to govern the practice of education in both religion studies and moral decision-making, as indeed in any other field, is the principle of education without indoctrination, or the principle of non-indoctrination. Indoctrination, as I use the term, is the opposite of education because it thwarts or hinders the free exercise of the mind which it is the business of education to develop. To indoctrinate, according to a recent dictionary, is to teach someone "to accept a system of thought uncritically."[1] When a person is given false information, or facts which constitute only one side of a story, he is thereby prevented from forming an intelligent opinion for himself. In any society, therefore, in which the ideal of education is held as a value at all, and I take this to be a basic commitment of a free society, indoctrination is not acceptable. As Supreme Court Justice Jackson once put it: "if there is any fixed star in our constitutional constellation, it is that no official, high or petty, can prescribe what shall be orthodox in politics, nationalism, religion, or other matters of opinion or force citizens to confess by word or act their Faith therein."[2] If we believe we are truly educating people, it is important for us to do all we can to insure against thwarting or coercing their opinions or decisions.

15

Without going into the background here, let me simply state what I take to be the basic principle of non-indoctrination.[3] The principle has two forms: first, we could not be said to be indoctrinating anyone if we are teaching something as true to which virtually no one objects. Thus children are not indoctrinated when they are taught latin verb forms, (as they used to be taught), the multiplication tables (which are still taught in some remote cor-ners), or the laws of Newtonian mechanics, without at the same time being taught that these are matters on which they should form their own opinions. The second form of the principle of non-indoctrination refers to those areas in which there is not complete agreement on the truth or credibility of the subject matter. Here the principle requires simply that where there is a difference of opinion students be taught that there is a difference of opinion. If people do not agree, for example, on the causes of the civil war, the moral acceptability of euthansaia, or the truth of Christian doctrine, students ought to be taught that these differences of infor-med opinion exist.

Having a clear principle of non-indoctrination is important to education in fields such as morality and religion studies in two ways. First of all, it operates as an educational criterion and can help teachers to decide what is and what is not acceptable practice. Secondly, however, when teachers are clear about what they are and are not expected to do educationally, they can do a better job of explaining their educational objectives to the general public or to those who have legal responsibility to education. In the work of the Moral Education Curriculum Development Project, we have found our efforts continually guided by the principle of non-indoctrination and have discovered that it helps us to reassure those who have doubts or questions about what we are doing.

Although the principle can be quite helpful to our efforts to formulate objectives and criteria in both moral education and relig-ion studies, I do not mean to imply that this formulation is in any way comprehensive or complete. It is, in fact, a principle which covers the cognitive domain only, leaving quite open the question of what we ought or ought not to be attempting educationally in the affective area. In discussion of this point, Professor Nicholas Piediscalzi has insisted that we must come to grips with the non-verbal and the "trans-rational," and I would certainly agree. Educators are responsible not only for the rational content at their teaching, but for whatever they bring youngsters to feel and be-lieve. And even without going into the difficult area of non-verbal communication, we shall first have to take seriously the "affective effects" of the objective study of religion and morality. It seems clear to me, and I would expect to others engaged in the academic study of religion, that university courses with whatever objective neutrality we might attempt to give them do have the effect of

attracting, repelling, expanding or diminishing students' faith
commitments. We must, in short, take account of what we are doing educationally despite what we think and say we are attempting
to do.

And what, furthermore, should we do when the criteria of non-
indoctrination seem to conflict with what are generally recognized
as the rights of parents in our society? Consider, for example, the
following educational objective:

> It is the proper business of the school to help
> the student choose some religion or irreligion,
> whichever one he wishes, for the living of his
> life, and to that end the school should set before
> him the various options.[4]

This objective would seem to follow directly from my second form
of the principle of non-indoctrination (that the alternatives be presented where differences of opinion exist) together with the presumably unobjectionable educational aim of teaching young people the
important place religion (or moral commitment) holds in the lives
of many people. Helping students to choose a religion or irreligion,
however, would certainly be objectionable to many parents. But
perhaps this objective would not be covered by principle of non-
indoctrination as it stands because teaching youngsters the "important place" of religion in people's lives moves us into the
affective realm, i.e. into belief or commitment, even though it
might be formulated as a cognitive objective. This problem does
show, however, that from a philosophy of education perspective the
principle of non-indoctrination as I have formulated it is inadequate
to our needs because it is limited to cognitive education. We need
now to raise the question of affective indoctrination to compliment
and extend the criteria. The approach of attempting to establish a
philosophically clear concept of education without indoctrination is
sound, I believe, and it is very useful for some problems; but it
needs to be extended beyond the cognitive realm and we shall have
to be careful to apply the "law" only within its own jurisdiction.[5]

THE NATURE OF MORAL EDUCATION

Let me now return to my thesis in somewhat of a round-about
manner by speaking first of the nature of moral education. This is
necessary because my own understanding of moral education differs
somewhat from other perspectives with which you may be familiar.
One of these perspectives, the psychological approach avanced
most prominently by the Harvard/Carnegie-Mellon project, is
based upon the notion that moral decisions are produced some-
where in the deep recesses or structures of the mind, which
seems to imply that morality has very little to do with conscious

18.

rational thought. While it is held by these theorists that the human mind does develop or progress through various stages or perspectives so that some form of moral education is possible, it is widely assumed that what is needed to facilitate moral development is merely experience in decision-making. Theorists of this school have generally denied the idea that there are any rational skills of decision-making which could be taught in a direct fashion. We can therefore designate this the "indirect" approach to moral education.

Another school of thought found often under the titles "humanistic" or "values clarification" seems to assume that decision-making is simply a matter of stating personal preferences. Moral development can be facilitated, according to this perspective, if educational techniques are developed which will help people to become clearer about their own preferences or values. Decision-making is thereby identified with "valuing", and moral development with knowing one's own mind or feelings more fully or clearly.

While there is something essential in each of these perspectives, the position we have taken[6] is that morality, or the moral point of view, is something more than either a person's stage or perspective, or his personal preferences. Morality, in our view, is best understood basically as decision-making although we would naturally draw a distinction between a person's more important decisions as his "moral" ones and his less important or "practical" ones. A person's decision-making is certainly the product of his stage of thought or perspective, and involves his personal preferences as well. But it also includes certain intellectual skills or abilities, such as the ability to understand the feelings of others, the ability to foresee the consequences of actions, the ability to imagine alternative courses of action from which to choose, the ability to complare one case or decision with another, and the ability to recognize and use common moral concepts. Our approach, therefore, is based upon the philosophical position that moral decision-making requires certain intellectual skills and that these are skills which can be taught. The teaching of principles or values as such, we believe, should be understood as the teaching of the nature and use of moral concepts; but equally if not more important in the facilitation of moral growth is the teaching of the skills and abilities necessary for clear thinking and decision-making. Our approach, therefore, might be designated a "direct" or philosophical one, at least by contrast to other theories.

From this perspective, we would consider the psychological or indirect approach deficient in its assumption that intellectual skills or abilities will develop naturally with experience as a person matures. To use the Piagetian model, this would be to assume that as a child's conception of reality develops through the various stages from informal to formal thought, the child will naturally acquire intellectual skills such as mathematical reasoning without ever being taught these. The child's conception of reality is very important to mathematics education, of course, but so is specific instruction in addition, subtraction, multiplication, and division. We cannot give over education entirely to the natural development of cognitive structures. In moral education there is something to be taught – not a specific moral code, but the skills and concepts of moral reasoning.

This leads directly to my thesis: moral education and religion studies differ in that it is possible to conceive moral education as education in the skills and concepts of moral thought rather than as a separate content field of study. Moral questions arise in all areas of life and must therefore be dealt with in all academic fields. The skills of moral thought cut across traditional disciplinary boundries. Religion studies, in contrast to this, is much more a field of specific content for education than a matter of intellectual skills.

It may be, of course, that there are some skills of religious thinking which can be taught, but this a point which we shall have to debate as we become clearer about the definition of our field and the establishment of educational objectives. In some public schools in New Jersey Transcendental Meditation is now taught as a strictly secular intellectual skill, but the religious implications of this are being challenged in the courts. I should think, however, that most educators in the field of religion studies would formulate their objectives more in terms of content than as cognitive or affective skills.

There are also, of course, certain moral theories which constitute the content of most university courses in ethics. Those who are concerned with moral education in public schools today, however, are inclined to shy away from the teaching of ethical theories and to center more upon the development of moral thought or sensitivity. In religion studies, however, whether one considers world religions, religious literature, religion and society, or the history of religion, one thinks primarily of a certain body of knowledge as the substance of education – although we would certainly not want to characterize this knowledge as the mere memorization of facts, since it should include a deeper understanding of and even the ability to empathize with people of various religious perspectives.

In any case let me propose this as my first point: that religion studies and moral education are distinct in that religion studies is primarily a content area while moral education is best conceived as education in intellectual skills or abilities.

INTELLECTUAL "FIELDS"

A second distinction between moral education and religion studies will become apparent if we consider the way in which morality is often related to religion, (I say "often" because many people hold moral perspectives which are not based upon religious beliefs at all.) While I realize that this is not the only way to picture the situation, let me suggest that we consider practical decision-making to be a common human function, some decisions to be much more important than others, and some decisions to be of such importance that we would consider them "moral" decisions, or what Professor R. M. Hare has called "decisions of principle."[7] Beyond these decisions of principle (and I am now still thinking of a hierarchy of intellectual functions) we find the principles or values themselves to which an individual would say he is ultimately committed. And I hope it is not too much of a distortion to say that religious believers generally see these values or principles as either products of, or essential aspects of their religious convictions. I would also hope that people who do not count themselves religious believers would be willing to agree that their values or principles are based upon, or "seated in," some type of world-view or paradigm of reality to which they are ultimately committed. Religion, of course, includes beliefs which go beyond "moral" beliefs and which are assertions about the nature of the world or the universe and which often involve the transcendent or supernatural. But for my purposes here, I do not need to say much more about the nature of this religious domain.[8] It might be noted, however, that my model would also leave room for those religious "believers" who consider religion to be essentially a moral world-view: I would hope that it might even seem fair to those who now argue that religious beliefs ought to be as much influenced by sensitive moral decision-making as decisions are by prior beliefs.

Given this model of intellectual functions from decision-making through values and principles to religious beliefs, I take it to be the business of moral education to deal with the lower half of the continuum: the values that people hold and the decisions which follow from these. Our own approach to moral education, in fact, is to begin at the very bottom, with concrete decisions, and to move from these toward the values upon which they are based. Religion, on the other hand, seems to me to deal with the basic beliefs people hold about the nature of the universe and, as it moves downward toward the practical, to show how the values or principles people hold are a consequence of their religious beliefs. It would appear from this model, therefore, that moral education and religion studies would each take up where the other leaves off. The two fields, it might be noted, are thus distinct although interdependent in the sense that either would naturally lead into the other.

Although I should want to speak of any division between these two fields as entirely artificial in the sense that the intellectual enterprise in either field cannot be limited or restricted to one half of the continuum without seriously crippling its effort, it does seem to me that the division is a natural one, and that it is quite possible and even rather practical to adopt it for educational purpose. Divisions such as this are common within the field of religion between theology and ethics, for example, or between theology and history. The distinction of intellectual fields is, of course, common in other areas of human learning. Biology and chemistry could certainly be placed on the same continuum although, for intellectual and academic purposes we customarily separate the two.

The reason for the development of these distinctions in the evolution of our intellectual ecology is not really obscure. Professor Stephen Toulmin has recently given an impressive account of the independent but interrelated development of various "fields" of knowledge as clusters of concepts around different practical concerns which have been or become central for people at different times and places. An intellectual discipline, according to Toulmin, "comprises a changing 'population' of concepts, and families of concepts, that are in general logically independent of one another."[9]

This is perhaps even more true today than in the past of religion and morality. Moral philosophy has been going its own way since the middle of last century and has, along with law, political philosophy, and history, developed its own conceptual tools for dealing with practical issues. Professor Hare, for example, limits his area of concern to talking about "decisions of principle," values, and ideals,[10] while at the same time acknowledging that the "nearest attempts" to the complete specification of ideal ways of life "are those given by the great religions."[11] Other philosophers, of course, insist that hierarchy ends with autonomous moral principles which are not necessarily related to any world-view religious or otherwise.[12] Without implying, however, that religion and morality are not related, I would say that I think there is enough intellectual independence in each field that treating them together is, at least for pedagogical purposes, more confusing, than helpful.

In contemporary philosophy it is not too difficult to maintain the independence of ethics from religion or even from metaphysics, since contemporary moral philosophers seem to be equally uninterested in both. The separation of religious morality or moral theology from religious belief is undoubtedly more questionable, but even here we seem to have developed considerable independence and academic autonomy although it would be difficult to demonstrate this conclusively. If we stay with Toulmin's analysis, we should look for the independent development and use of concepts, but I should think that recent claims of the influence of ethics upon belief such as

22.

that offered by Dr. Barbara Swyhart would also support the independence of religious moral thought.[13]

Moral Education and Religion Studies, therefore, ought to be considered separate educational tasks because they are sufficiently separate or autonomous intellectual disciplines. Moral Philosophy, at any rate, is autonomous and there are many moral perspectives which are not based upon religious beliefs.

SOME LEGAL CONSIDERATIONS

A third reason for the separation of moral education and religion studies arises from consideration of recent Supreme Court decisions regarding religion and the public schools. The point I would like to make is that the courts have already and, I believe, will continue to treat these fields in separate ways.

Religion has been dealt with as a field of academic study and has been defended by the Supreme Court as an appropriate part of the public school curriculum. Mr. Justice Clark's statements in the Schempp case are often quoted: "Nothing we have said here indicates that such study of the Bible or of religion, when presented objectively as part of a secular program of education, may not be effected consistently with the First Amendment."[14] The issue was more directly considered, however, in the Supreme Court of Washington where the teaching of the historical and literary aspects of the Bible was challenged by fundamentalist churches and clergy. In Calvary Bible Presbyterian Church v. Board of Regents the court held that:

> the framers of our constitution did not intend
> the word "instruction" to be construed without
> limit, but that the proscribed field be confined
> to that category of instruction that resembles
> worship and manifests a devotion to religion and
> religious principles in thought, feeling, belief,
> and conduct, i.e., instruction that is devotional
> in nature and designed to induce faith and belief
> in the student. There can be no doubt that our
> constitutional bars are absolute against religious
> instruction and indoctrination in specific religious
> beliefs or dogma; but they do not proscribe open,
> free, critical and scholarly examination of the
> literature, experiences, and knowledge of mankind.[15]

While there are still many difficulties with this position, since for example it might seem to limit religion studies more or less to the cognitive domain, it is a much clearer position than the courts have ever taken with regard to moral education. Moral education

is legally a different matter since, in so far as moral education may
be considered a secular matter (and I shall not attempt to say how
far this is), it does seem that the public schools are constitutionally
permitted and even under the mandate of certain executive and legis-
lative statements actively to promote belief in and commitment to
certain values often identified as social or democratic ideals. Moral
education can, therefore, not only enter into the affective domain,
but it has long been stated that one purpose or objective of public
education is to exercise a moral influence upon students to the
benefit of our democratic society. There is furthermore, I believe,
a conflict brewing in the field of moral education between a public
which largely favors direct inculcation if not indoctrination in
national values and educators committed to the educational principle
of non-indoctrination who are preparing to teach youngsters to think
for themselves.

This conflict, at any rate, as well as other constitutional guidance for moral education will be governed, in my opinion, not by
decisions such as Schempp and the Calvary Presbyterian Bible
Church but by decisions concerning loyalty oaths or pledges such as
the compulsorary flag salute case in West Virginia. In this case
Mr. Justice Jackson held that although states may even "require
teaching ... of all in our history and in the structure and organization of our government ... which tend to inspire patriotism and love
of country (emphasis mine)," it may not compel students to declare
a belief by a salute or pledge.[16] Justice Jackson's distinction is a
subtle and important one with many implications; my point is, however, that it assumes that the state does have a right to "inspire"
patriotism (he also uses the phrase "aroused loyalties") which is
certainly one form of commitment to a moral position. In contrast
to the "wall of separation" considerations which govern religion
studies, therefore, moral educators face both judicial and legisla-
tive traditions which tend to favor the "inculcation" of beliefs, feelings, and commitments -- the very affects proscribed for religion
studies.

From the legal perspective, therefore, the aims and objectives
of moral education and religion studies will differ as required by the
constitution and this is a very strong reason for educators to treat
the two as separate fields.

SOME PRACTICAL CONSIDERATIONS

My final reason for upholding a strong distinction between
moral education and religion studies is of a much more practical
nature, although it is an important point of educational theory. I
believe that we shall simply do a lot better job of both moral educa-

tion and religion studies and we will be better able to explain our activities as educators to the general public and their elected representatives on school boards if we treat these as separate fields.

From a point of view of education criteria, and with regard to the principle of non-indoctrination in particular, the separation of moral education from religion studies will help educators formulate their objectives more clearly. The criterion of non-doctrination would, of course, have to be applied to both fields. There are a number of major religious belief systems in the world today and religion studies teachers will have to assure themselves intellectually that they are presenting each fairly. (Personally I am inclined to think this educational criterion is violated by curriculum offerings which contain courses only in Bible Literature without mention of the literature of other religions.) And moral education teachers will have to take care both that they do not present any particular code of rules or decisions as moral absolutes, and that their discussion of value orientations is not biased or restricted. Since there are these two crucial areas, religious belief systems and value orientations, in which we will have to be especially conscious of avoding indoctrination, therefore, I think it would be much easier to develop adequate teaching methods and curricular materials if educators concentrate upon only one at a time.

This might not be as important if there were a one to one correspondence between distinct belief systems and recognizably different value orientations. This is not the case, however. There is a good deal of "cross-over" between religious beliefs and moral perspectives. The major religious denominations in our society seem each to have their liberal and conservative wings, and the liberals or the conservatives of different denominations are likely to have more in common by the way of moral perspective than one can find within any given denomination. I would think it especially advisable, therefore, to formulate educational aims and approaches for religion studies and moral education independently.

Let me suggest, therefore, what might be called the "Public Relations" argument. Public relations arguments carry a lot of weight these days which I generally like to resist; but in this case it is based upon the notion that if we can formulate our educational objectives and criteria clearly, we shall be more effective in the public domain, which is, after all, where policy for public school education must ultimately be justified. Since we are talking primarily about public education, therefore, it is important that we take care to be able to explain our aims and objectives clearly. The public relations argument against the formulation of aims and objectives in ways which are needlessly confusing is in this case, therefore, a forceful and a valid one.

In attempting to describe moral education to people, John Davis and I have often said that we intend to deal with the development of decision-making skills and moral concepts by moving from matters which are very practical toward matters of principle or value. We hope that we can give sufficient recognition to the variety of value stances that exist in our society and to show that there are differences of opinion on specific moral questions, while at the same time showing that values or principles are very important for decision-making and are thus important in the development of morally coherent life-styles. That is, we wish to emphasize the importance of values and principles without indoctrinating young people into any single set of moral beliefs or decisions. We have said, furthermore, that although we recognize that people's values are based upon their religious views (or, as the case may be, upon humanistic world-views), we do not consider it the business of moral education to deal with the foundations of people's values in their religious or scientific beliefs. In saying that for the purposes of moral education we draw a line at this point, we have also said that we hope to show complete respect for people's religious views and to acknowledge, without distortion, the important place religion plays in the development of moral life-styles. We have found, furthermore, that many people do believe this to be a reasonable way of going about our task. It is one, however, which helps us to indicate that we are not in the business of "religious education" (as distinguised from religion studies). Drawing the line at this point allows us, in short, to say fairly clearly what it is we intend to do and thereby to convince others that we do have a reasonably clear idea of the place of moral education in the public school curriculum.

It would seem that a similar advantage would be gained by people engaging in religion studies in public education if they draw the same artificial line that we have used. It would be easier to make it clear, it seems to me, that we are advocating the academic study of religion and not teaching any particular religious faith commitment or any religious moral perspective. This would, however, allow the educator in religion studies to go as far as showing how different value commitments are related to, or based upon, different religious perspectives. And I would think it a very important part of religion studies to show how beliefs influence people's behavior by influencing the value commitments they make. The religion studies teacher would still be dealing with a variety of value positions and would not be in danger of indoctrinating unless, of course, he presented one value position and religion to the exclusion of others. At the same time, however, he would be able to explain that his field deals with the major beliefs that people hold and does not, to any great extent at least, get into the realm of personal moral decisions. If teachers in this field are able to say that they are drawing the line at this point it may help to alay people's fears that the teaching of religion in public schools will become a covert teaching of specific moral positions, and this is the major objection many people have to religion studies in public schools. Religion studies would benefit from keeping these two fields separate, therefore, in the same way that we feel that we have benefitted in moral education. We believe that we have developed a fairly coherent rationale for moral education, but I would not like to have to explain the aims and objectives of religion studies every time I present this rationale. It is not that we could not present both fields; but that the fields differ in nature and objective, and by the time one has accomplished both, people are usually confused. The fact that the aims and objectives of public education in these two fields differ and that a different rationale is required for each is reason enough to keep the two field separate in practice.

Finally I would like to emphasize the importance of developing in these fields clear and persuasive accounts of what educators are proposing and doing. And an important aspect of each rationale will be a sharp distinction between education which builds understanding of the various moral and religious positions held by people and indoctrination which attempts to present one position to the exclusion of others.

There are many people in our society, however, who will still object to this. They want their own religious beliefs to be taught as true regardless of the fact that many people do not hold them. They want moral decisions and values to be taught as absolutes regardless of the fact that people disagree about these. In order to establish good education in both of these areas, therefore, educators will have to make it clear that it is not their business to indoctrinate. If an educator does not present one religious position fairly or as strongly as it might be, then he is guilty of giving a false impression of the state of human knowledge in the field of religion. If a moral educator does not present one set of value commitments in the way it deserves, then he too is guilty of presenting less than the full truth. On the other hand, if people wish their own religious beliefs or their own moral values to be presented as absolutely true, then educators must make it clear that it is they and not the educators who are proposing to indoctrinate.

FOOTNOTES

1.   *The American Heritage Dictionary of the English Language.*
     New York: The American Heritage Publishing Co., 1969.
     p. 671.

2.   *West Virginia State Board of Education v. Barnette.*
     63 S. Ct. at page 1187. (319 U. S. 624).

3.   For an analysis and defense of this position see R. T. Hall
     and J. U. Davis, *Moral Education in Theory and Practice.*
     Buffalo, New York: Prometheus Books, 1975, Ch. 2. The
     most important essays on the concept of indoctrination are
     collected in I. A. Snook, ed., *Concepts of Indoctrination.*
     London: Routledge and Kegan Paul, 1972 and in T. H. B.
     Hollins, ed., *Aims in Education.* Manchester, England:
     Manchester University Press,1964.

4.   This aim is presented as a "customarily adduced" justifica-
     tion of religion studies by Nicholas Wolterstorff in "Neutral-
     ity and Impartiality," in T. R. Sizer, ed., *Religion and
     Public Education.* Boston: Houghton Mifflin Co., 1967, p.19.

5.   Affective Indoctrination has yet to receive much direct or
     systematic attention from philosophers of education. I have
     attempted some tentative suggestions, however, in a lecture,
     "On Indoctrination" which will be published in John Geiger,
     ed., *Values and Rights in Public Education* (forthcoming).

6.   R. T. Hall and John U. Davis, *Moral Education in Theory
     and Practice.*

7.   R. M. Hare, *The Language of Morals.* Oxford: Oxford
     University Press,1952, Ch. 4.

8.   In this context I am thinking in terms of a sociological
     definition of "religion" rather than one formulated from
     within any single religious perspective. Cf. Roland Robert-
     son, *The Sociological Interpretation of Religion.* New York:
     Schocken Books, 1970, pp. 34 – 50.

9.   Stephen Toulmin, *Human Understanding,* Vol. 1. Oxford:
     Oxford University Press, 1972, p. 134.

10. R. M. Hare, *Freedom and Reason.* Oxford: Oxford Univer-
     sity Press, 1963, Chs. 3 and 8.

28.

11. R. M. Hare, The Language of Morals. p. 69.

12. See A. Phillips Griffiths, "Ultimate Moral Principles:
    Their Justification," in P. Edwards, ed., The Encyclopedia
    of Philosophy. New York: Macmillan, 1967, Vol. 8,
    pp. 177 – 182.

13. Barbara Ann DeMartino Swyhart, Bioethical Decision –
    Making. Philadelphia: Fortress Press, 1975.

14. School District of Abington Township, Pennsylvania v.
    Schempp. 83 S. Ct. at page 1573. 374 U. S. 203 (1963).

15. 436 P. 2d, 189 at page 193.

16. West Virginia State Board of Education v. Barnette.
    63 S. Ct. 1178 at page 1182. 319 U. S. 624.

The Paradox of Moral/Values Education and Religion-Studies: A Critical Overview*

Barbara Ann Swyhart, Ph.D.
Visiting Lecturer, Director
Program on Religion and
  Education, Harvard University
The Divinity School, 1975-76

Associate Professor
Coordinator of Religion and
  Public Education
Dept. of Religious Studies
San Diego State University

This essay is written for the purpose of describing the diverse psychological, philosophical and sociological theories of moral education, values education, moral development, and values clarification toward the discussion of the distinctions among them and their relationship to the academic study of religion in public education. The focus of the overview is the formulation of a set of guidelines for the clarification of the discipline of religion-studies in relation to moral/values education. The immediate direction of this presentation is a critical description of the methodologies and methods (in theory and practice) presently influencing public education. It will focus primarily on American methodologies although the British approach has both influenced some American methodologies as well as contributed in its own right to moral theory. For the most part I will refer to British sources as they reflect sources of influence on American theorists and practitioners of moral/values education.

At the conclusion I will suggest a rationale for a methodology which will coordinate the various efforts in these two fields. A selected bibliography is also made available. A supplementary listing of moral/values education projects and/or centers is also available in the Appendix.

Four questions underlie the direction of this study: 1) Why is moral/values education necessary and/or important? 2) Who is addressed by moral/values education? 3) What is accomplished in moral/values education? 4) What specific distinctions obtain between moral/values education and the academic study of religion in public education?

*I wish to thank Bob Hall, Director of the Moral Education Project, the College of Steubenville, for his critical reading, and valuable editorial comments, of the first draft of this essay.

1 Prologue: Some Legal Considerations

The present legal situation within the American educational system which gives rise to our concern with this topic develops from ambiguous and often paradoxical (sometimes contradictory) statements in past Supreme Court decisions with regard to religion, and morality. Although it is most emphatically clear that one may teach about religion in an academic context, rather than teach religion,[1] it is not as clear what the Supreme Court has meant by its endorsement of teaching, or at least "asserting morality or moral values."[2] Presumably this might refer to "the bag of virtues" approach under critical scrutiny by Lawrence Kohlberg and his associates at the Center for Moral Development, Harvard University, among others. However, the problem is much larger and involves the complex problematic of the paradox of religion and morality in American civil life. Justice Brennan states the paradox very well in his concurrent opinion in the Schempp/Murray decision of 1963 which is the Supreme Court decision quoted in the liberation of the academic study of religion. This paradox reminds us of the very cogency of the problem under discussion. It is also a key to providing the primary national issue in moral/values education - the "rights of conscience" - in public education, including the ramifications of this issue in both the individual and the public domains.

> When John Locke ventured in 1689, "I esteem it above all things necessary to distinguish exactly the business of civil government from that of religion and to settle the just bounds that lie between the one and the other," he anticipated the necessity which would be thought by the Framers to require the adoption of the First Amendment, but not the difficulty that would be experienced in defining those "just bounds." The fact is that the line which separates the secular from the sectarian in American life is elusive. The difficulty of defining the boundary with precision inheres in a paradox central to our schema of liberty. While our institutions reflect a firm conviction that we are a religious people, those institutions by solemn constitutional injunction may not officially involve religion in such a way as to prefer, discriminate against, or oppress a particular sect or religion. Equally the Constitution enjoins those involvements of religious with secular institutions which a) serve the essentially religious activities of religious institutions; b) employ the organs of government for essentially religious means to serve governmental ends where secular means would suffice. The constitutional mandate expresses a deliberate and considered judgment that such matters are to be left to the conscience of the citizen, and declares

as a basic postulate of the relation between the citizen and his government that "the rights of conscience are, in their nature, of peculiar delicacy, and will bear little the gentlest touch of governmental hand...."3

Thayer Warshaw has unfolded this problem further in his Religion, Public Education, the Supreme Court in a discussion of Welsh vs. U.S. (1970).

> If the Court's definition of religious beliefs applied here, and its definition of God in Seegar -- both used to construe the Military Service statute - were to be applied consistently by the Court to "religion" in the First Amendment, a public school teacher would face a dilemma. Schools are expected to foster moral values (Pierce 1925), but may not foster religion. If the teacher believes in the moral values she/he teaches, and if purely moral beliefs -- divorced from God, sect, and ritual -- constitute religious beliefs, then the teacher cannot foster moral values without fostering religious beliefs. Moral values would be considered a part of or sanctioned by "religious" beliefs and could not stand apart from religion. As Burger said in the Lemon case (1971), "what would appear to some to be essential to good citizenship might well to others border on or constitute instruction in religion."4

In both statements the paradox of morality and religion vis à vis "the rights of conscience" is disclosed. Two distinct concerns are linked together, not by content, but by the intensity of their human impact because of the inseparability in the minds of many people of moral and religious values. To clarify the source of Mr. Warshaw's concern, reflection on U.S. vs. Seegar, (1965) in a case of conscientious objection, reveals that the Supreme Court allowed exemptions on the basis of Justice Clark's interpretation "in a relation to a Supreme Being" in the draft law (changed from God in the earlier versions of the statute)) as a "belief that is sincere and meaningful (and) occupies a place in the life of its possessor parallel to that filled by the orthodox belief in God of one who clearly qualifies for the exemption." Using Tillich's definition of God, he further said: "Translate it (i.e. "God") and speak of the depths of your life, the source of your being, of your ultimate concern, of what you take seriously without reservation."5

The ambiguity between any strictly defined sense of religion and what one takes ultimately "not including essentially political, sociological, or philosophical views on a merely personal moral code," seriously forces us to question the relationship between a sense of personal value, and "religion" as both touch the legal rights of individuals. For this Warshaw refers us to

two cases: Pierce (1925) and Torcaso (1961). In Pierce
vs. Society of Sisters, Justice McReynolds emphasized
"that teachers be of good moral character and patriotic
disposition, that certain studies plainly essential to
good citizenship be taught, and that nothing be taught
that is manifestly inimical to the public welfare." In
Torcaso vs. Watkins the Court wrote a most important
footnote to a case in which a Maryland law required a
profession of belief in the existence of God before one
could hold a public office to be unconstitutional. That
footnote (note 11) indicates that "among religions in
this country which do not teach what would generally be
considered a belief in the existence of a God are
Buddhism, Taoism, Ethical Culture, and others." The
problem is again addressed by Warshaw:

> The Court's remarks about the "good moral
> character and patriotic disposition" of
> teachers and about "studies plainly essential
> to good citizenship" are of interest to
> peoples concerned with the teaching of values
> in public schools. The Court has repeatedly
> acknowledged the schools right and
> responsibility toward the "secular formation
> of moral values." Which values are religious
> values depends on one's definition of religion
> (See Welch, 1970). As to tests of a teacher's
> "good moral character and patriotic disposition"
> and criteria of "good citizenship," the Court
> has issued no definitions for school boards to
> follow, although it has generally subscribed
> to the principle that for the individual there
> may be a moral power higher than the State.
> How far to extend the criteria for teaching
> that may be "inimical to the public welfare"
> can be a matter of considerable debate among
> educators and educational pressure groups.[6]

In addition to the ultimate relation of morality and
religion suggested by the coupling of these disciplines,
it is suggested that a secular approach to morals is
indeed possible. This possibility confronts Boards of
Education, Social Education and Social Science specialists,
as well as teachers of Humanities as the imperative for
moral education and character training is randomly
initiated by local schools. Briefly there are two
distinct problems which must be faced. The first is the
legal paradox of conscience formation via moral education
and the second is the prohibition against indoctrination
of any kind (especially religious) acknowledging allowance
for teaching about religion. Morality, however, does
not have the legal caution against indoctrination as
religion does. What then is the crucial issue in the
relationship of moral education to the rights of
conscience? One text, Moral Education: Interdisciplinary
Approaches raises the question of a "content-free
methodology of morals,"[7] comprising both aspects of the
problem: 1) the question of a sound methodology, and
2) a value-free methodology. The first aspect involves

us in an investigation of what psychological and   33.
philosophical theories and approaches are presently in
use. The second, i.e. the possibility of a value-free
methodology, has to do with the inculcation of enabling
activities geared to the development of moral reasoning
in the child without coercion by subtle persuasion into
or in a specific moral stance. The tension between these
two aspects is the crux of the problematic of moral/values
education as its legal relationship to religion-studies
is understood and articulated.

II   Approaches to Moral/Values Education

There are presently at work diverse methodologies
in use in projects and classroom activities. The
methodologies are justified by theoretical models and
rationale. The first notable model is the developmental
psychological approach of Lawrence Kohlberg. He has
structured six stage of child development (following
the model of Piaget) with regard to morality and
conscience. His view of morality, however, is predicated
upon a revitalized Platonic world view of "the good" but
contra the Aristolelian "bag of virtues."

> The objection of the psychologist to the bag
> of virtues is that there are no such things.
> Virtues and vices are labels by which people
> award praise or blame to others, but the ways
> people use praise and blame toward others are
> not the ways in which they think when making
> moral decisions themselves.[8]

Instead of the "bag of virtues" approach Kohlberg adopts
the values under justice as the proper content of moral
education. He claims that the problem which is
addressed in this paper would disappear with the
adoption of the single concept of justice as the
authentic rationale and content for moral education.
Kohlberg states:

> The problems as to the legitimacy of moral
> education in the public schools disappear,
> however, if the proper content of moral
> education is recognized to be the values of
> justice which themselves prohibit the
> imposition of beliefs of one group upon
> another. The requirement implied by the
> Bill of Rights is that the schools are not
> to be value-oriented. Recognition of equal
> rights does not imply value neutrality, i.e.
> the view that all value systems are equally
> sound. Because we respect the individual
> rights of members of particular groups in
> our society, it is sometimes believed that
> we must consider their values as valid as
> our own.[9]

Kohlberg's perception of the meaning of "value neutrality"
is subject to much constructive criticism. Nevertheless,

his perception had led to the development of a moral
principle, which is "a mode of choosing which is
universal, a rule of choosing which we want all people
to adopt always in all situations."[10] This, he says,
is the nature of justice. Kohlberg rejects a
"relativistic" notion of value neutrality--but is that
its only possible expression?

The scheme which Kohlberg develops, based on cross-
cultural studies, is a series of moral "orientations" or
"perspectives" which constitute a developmental sequence
in moral education. This sequence suggests a diverse
form of moral education for children, distinct from the
"ethical relativity" of adults. The six stages
consisting of pre-conventional, conventional and post-
conventional structures are characterized by 1) the
invariance of the sequence; 2) the "structured wholes"
or "total ways of thinking" which children develop as
opposed to mere attitudes toward particular situations; 3)
"a stage concept (which) implies universality of
sequences under varying cultural conditions."[11] He
argues that sound "scientific notions of the cultural
relativity of morals" are false. Further, (he claims)
"that basic moral principles are dependent upon a
particular religion, or any religion at all," is also
a false notion.[12]

> We have found no important differences in the
> development of moral thinking between
> (among) Catholics, Protestants, Jews,
> Buddhists, Moslems, and atheists. Children's
> moral values in the religious area seem to
> go through the same stages as their general
> moral values so that a stage-two child is
> likely to say "Be good to God and he'll be
> good to you." Both cultural values and
> religion are important factors in
> selectively elaborating certain themes in
> the moral life but they are not unique
> causes of the development of basic moral
> values. Our data does not indicate that all
> values are universal, but rather that basic
> moral values are universal. (emphasis mine) [13]

A natural yet developmental approach to moral education
is suggested. Religion may supply "themes in the moral
life," but not the foundation or necessity of values.
What is accomplished by Kohlberg is the creation of a
hierarchical schema of levels and stage development
based on universal levels of moral behavior.

A number of critics have argued that Professor
Kohlberg's work has only partially disclosed the
problematic of moral education. R.S. Peters has
suggested that "how" morality is used does not say what
morality is; that the Kantian imperative is not the only
approach to morality; that universality is highly
suspect.[14] He further suggests that both Piaget and
Kohlberg are missing the affective domain dealing with
"guilt, other-relatedness and so on."[15] Professor Peters
also states that, while Kohlberg sees the importance of

will in morality he does not give evidence of how to   35.
foster its development as an educational objective.[16]
     Still another perspective, - the Socio-Political
Perspective - one which initiated the urgent look at the
youth of the 60's, is that of Kenneth Keniston and his
discourse on alienation and modern youth, The
Uncommitted.[17] In a more recent article, Professor
Keniston adds a dimension to Professor Kohlberg's
observations. He says:

> In any discussion of moral education, then,
> we should of course consider the general
> stages in the development of moral reasoning,
> its alleged familial preconditions, and the
> logic and technique of moral education. But,
> in addition, we need to examine the particular
> moral problems that today concern us and the
> context in which today's moral dilemmas arise,
> for morality is not only a matter of how
> children are brought up, are educated, and
> learn to reason but -- in the crunch -- a
> matter of what they believe, what they are
> willing to act on, and how they define the
> world in which they live. Professor Kohlberg's
> work suggests that many of those who today
> experience the greatest sense of personal
> moral crisis are those whose moral reasoning
> places them in obvious conflict with the
> majority of Americans who think in more
> conventional ways and inevitably confuse
> past with preconventional moral thinking.
> However illuminating such analyses are, they
> still do not speak specifically to the urgent
> sense of moral crisis of our own time. They
> do not tell us why, in this particular epoch
> in American (and world) history, the sense of
> moral crisis should be so intense, nor do
> they speak to those more specific moral
> questions, values and orientations which
> today seem challenged or which today are used
> to challenge existing institutions and values.
> Finally, they do not explain why today the
> most intense moral challenges to the existing
> order come from the young.[18]

Moral education, in Keniston's view, will be ineffective
unless it takes the basic problem of our socio-political
culture into account as its setting or context.
     In apparent agreement with Keniston's perspective,
Donald Oliver and M.J. Bane suggest an alternative to
Kohlberg's theory in terms of the use of "value conflict"
in the classroom. "The basic value premise of the
curriculum may be called 'rational consent,' the implicit
agreement that controversy is to be accommodated or
resolved by reflection and conversation rather than force
or coercion."[19] Basically, their focus is the ability of
students to judge public policies in a socio-political
setting.[20] Moral reasoning, they believe, is not enough.
Strategies of justification and clarification including

the use of analogy, evaluating evidence, defining terms,
making distinctions and the discussion process itself are
part of the effort to simulate an environment of dissent
and challenge. Rather than disallowing Kohlberg's
psychological perspective, they build on developmental
psychology, the rational premises of S.I. Benn and R.S.
Peters,[21] and add a radical view of the educational
process in which complex reality should be faced in the
effort to create moral sensitivity "to paradox and
tragedy in human nature (rather than consistency and
universality in moral rules)...a far more powerful force
in the expression of man's inherent humanity than the
use of reasoning strategies in the development of flexible
moral principles."[22] Obviously both Professors Oliver
and Bane show genuine acceptance of violence and
contradiction in the public arena of moral confusion.
Innovative classes and curriculum are advocated.

> We believe, therefore, that great issues of the
> human spirit, such as feelings and expressions
> of violence, must be dealt with on a level
> deeper than that suggested by such phrases as
> "justification strategies" or "moral reasoning."
> We believe that education should encourage
> people to examine the relationships of men to
> their societies and to the universe not only
> through the rational analysis of "case studies,"
> but also through the genuine attempt to create
> and wonder about a profound, perhaps religious,
> experience.[23]

In still another context--in a study of three
different Jewish school settings--Mr. Sidney Selig and
Rabbi Gerald Teller tested Kohlberg's theory in two
different Conservative Congregational Schools and one
Traditional Day School. They concluded that from the
fourth to the sixth grades students move from a highly
legalistic position to a more individualistic one
stressing the person over the law. However, "the
researchers differ with Kohlberg in that they feel that
once children have moved to stage six, they may choose
various stages below stage six for religious or cultural
reasons. While Kohlberg posits that his stages are
universal, the researchers feel that they are cultural.
In American thinking, the highest virtue is individual
conscience. In Judaism, the highest value would be the
person as part of a committed community. Jews make moral
choices against a framework of halachah. Kohlberg would
deny that this is stage six thinking yet the researchers
assume that Kohlberg does not understand the underlying
foundations of a traditional faith. Autonomy for the
Jew is found not in individual consciences but through a
living relationship, with the halachic community."[24]
Thus cultural-religious expectation may alter the ultimate
goals of the moral life. Further, this is a primary
example of the difference between religious education and
religion-studies in public education. The former
evaluates a specific morality; the latter simply teaches
about moral perspectives.

The moral/values education issue has philosophical voices· as well. In addition to the developmental approach from the psychological perspective, there are additional philosophical dimensions. Among them are the cognitive approach,[25] and the affective domain, including values clarification.[26] Affective education is the particular emphasis of John R. Meyer and his Canadian Associates in values education.[27] Values clarification is a method usually employed toward affective education, but comprises an approach and characteristics in its own right. In addition, there is a rational approach which bridges the gap between the psychological model and the analytic, philosophical approach of John Wilson of the Farmington Trust Unit in Oxford, England. This approach is documented in Moral Education in Theory and Practice by Robert T. Hall and John Davis.[28] In considering each of these perspectives it is important to realize that there will be overlap of one perspective with another. However, I have tried to emphasize the obvious points of difference among these perspectives toward the focus of the relationship and distinction between moral/values education and religion-studies.

There is a radical disagreement between the affectivists and the cognitivists whether psychological or philosophical. The former, stressing an emotive, action-orientation and employing values clarification techniques, speaks to the cognitivist primarily with a relativistic voice, placing the consequence before the cause. The cognitivist says that affective education is "the last supplement in the pedagogy of ethics."[29] "First must come the legitimation of ethics itself, then the legitimation of moral education, then the cognitive structuring of moral education, then the teaching of the basic cognitive elements in ethics -- and only then the affect, the icing on the cake."[30]

The values clarification advocates are characteristically concerned with "personal choices." These choices, "if they are possibly to lead to values, must involve alternatives which 1) include ones that are prized by the chooser; 2) have meaning to the chooser, as when the consequence of each one are clearly understood; and 3) are freely available for selection."[31] Values and valuing are the result of a process of

A. Choosing (freely, from alternatives, after thoughtful consideration of the consequence of each alternative);

B. Prizing (cherishing, being happy with the choice; willing to affirm the choice publicly);

C. Acting (doing something with the choice; repeatedly, in some pattern of life).[32]

Certain functions of the human being are indicators of values. Goals, aspirations, attitudes, interest, feelings, beliefs and convictions, activities, worries, problems and obstacles become that which comes to the discussion as students face theoretically conceived conflict situations which are contrived to create and raise plural opinions as well as allow students to be conscious of their own and others' processes of valuing.[33]

At the other end of the philosophical spectrum is

the rational approach of Robert Hall and John Davis. The authors base their philosophical approach on the work of John Wilson. "The essence of Mr. Wilson's approach is that moral education should consist not in the teaching of any specific set of moral rules but in communicating a rational method which an individual can use to develop his own moral principles."[34] The rational method draws on both analytic philosophy and developmental psychology and centers on the whole person by creating an educational environment conducive to developing critical thinking skills.

The key to the theme and approach of the book is the premise that education without indoctrination is possible. The authors insist on the "avoidance of indoctrination" both as a procedural and substantive principle. Indoctrination is here defined as "a misrepresentation of the credibility of the subject being taught or as communicating or imparting knowledge without fairly or accurately indicating its credibility. In both cases, of course, the credibility of the facts or theories professed would have to be determined by an analysis of the knowledge situation as it is, that is, by ... empirical criterion...."[35] The "credibility" of the material puts the burden of the academic knowledge of the material on the teacher. It is precisely this professionalism which aids in the distancing of the teacher from the material so that no one moral perspective is given priority. Further, actual concrete cases are used as reference points for the analysis of the cognitive process involved in the moral domain. This concern with indoctrination is addressed by neither the values clarification advocates nor by the moral developmentalists because neither have directly addressed the philosophical issue of the moral domain. What Hall and Davis are suggesting is a reflective (rational) analysis of the nature of the moral itself, including moral judgments, principles, ideals and values as they can be articulated through practical, real-life situations. Teaching individual values--however noble and praiseworthy they may seem--simply fosters "a religion of public school morality (my term)," one-dimensional in scope and content. The authors do shed substantial doubt on the efficacy of such an approach as well agree with Kohlberg's criticism of the "bag of virtues" approach. They demonstrate that it is possible to teach the nature of the moral itself to high school students.

Although a cognitive developmental position is also advocated by the authors, a lengthy criticism of the Kohlberg Model if offered. They suggest that Kohlberg has a philosophical position, rather than simply a psychological one, and they are in radical disagreement with Kohlberg's philosophy. They also suggest that Kohlberg has not taken social learning or character traits into consideration in the formulation of the stages of moral growth; nor has he seriously considered the question of the transition from one stage to the other. Although both processes are concerned with the autonomy of the individual, Hall and Davis do disagree

with the description of justice expressed by Kohlberg
as the highest level in stage six. Hall and Davis
express what they see as Kohlberg's problem of
articulating one mode of morality instead of allowing
students to see, understand and analyze alternate models
of justice through reflection on the nature of the
construct "justice" itself.

There is a strong Kantian base to the approach of
Hall and Davis: Morality is its own justification;
when one adopts a moral perspective it becomes
universal in that it is the one he/she expects others
to follow. At times this thread is too thin and very
subtly expressed. In spite of a common beginning to
Hall and Davis, and Kohlberg, the essential difference
between them must be underlined: Kohlberg establishes
universal, structured, predictable stages of moral
development a priori; Hall and Davis work from actual
situations and decisions inducing the moral perspective
with a focus on the process of structured, cognitive
education in the moral domain.

Hall and Davis do raise critical concerns which
should be discussed for the purpose of justifying to
educators the feasibility, as well as the necessity, of
this approach. For example, I do feel that it will be
difficult for many to accept the principle of "education
without indoctrination" as it is for people to accept
"teaching about religion". However, I agree with Hall
and Davis that this approach is not only possible but
essential. A "morally neutral definition of morality"[36]
is the authors' response to our dilemma. Nevertheless,
how to educate teachers to this approach will be a major
enterprise.

A distinct concern which troubles me is their
definition of morality as "one's ultimate reasons for
acting."[37] What disturbs me is the use of the word
"ultimate" and then the dismissal of a consideration of
either the psychology of motivation or a philosophy of
intentionality which may render one reason more
appropriate than another. (Notice I did not say "one
reason 'right' and another 'wrong'.") Since I cannot
alter the authors' definition of morality I would suggest
that a logical and necessary follow up to the nature of
the moral might be an excursion into the realm of various
paradigms-of-reality suggested by religious, humanistic,
secular and other ideologies which in fact are the actual
attitudes, private and public, expressed or believed by
most individuals. The roots of the nature of the moral
are not to be found in paradigms. However, the psycho-
social motivations for moral expressions are indeed
evident in these ideologies. In other words, the
historical and psycho-social roots of the moral
imperative are important in the decision-making process
since often they are the realities of the moral taboos
and permissions in the first place. Relating this to the
process of intentionality which endow public expressions
of morality fosters an addition to the very sound
pedagogical process articulated by Hall and Davis. Yet I
would not speak of moral education at all--but rather of
education in ethics toward the decision-making process.

Morality presupposes a language of "right and wrong," "good and bad," appropriate only to imperatives derived from a source which is accepted as authoritatively true. Since education is not about the business of "moralizing morality," the process of education involves options presented by an ethician, or one knowledgeable and skilled in the art of ethical education.

The most crucial issue which Hall and Davis pose is the problem of choice and choosing among alternatives. It is not their intention to suggest a good or better or best solution to a dilemma. However, what happens when the student--no longer a product of the sixties with its total freedom--seeks a response of value to some of the very meaningful practical problems posed by the authors, such as drug use, abortion, etc.? Here we are reminded of Kenneth Keniston's concern with Kohlberg's approach. Unfortunately this need among students and teachers has made of the Kohlbergian approach an oasis of structure in the desert of freedom to do what one wants. The structures of his system are seized by religious and public institutions alike for the purpose of instilling a pattern of development--a motive to which I am sure Kohlberg would object. Content is readily found for each stage and this model is more appealing than the difficult analytic philosophical method entertained by the authors. However, while this may be the case for some from the practical point of view, I strongly urge that Hall and Davis be taken seriously as they articulate a more efficacious and self-fulfilling process for moral education. I would add an approach to ethical education via paradigms of reality within the context of religion-studies (including non-theistic, theistic, western, eastern, humanist, etc.).

A revival of the Socratic method wed to the analytic philosophy and developmental psychology advocated by Hall and Davis returns moral education to its primary concern--developing decision-making skills for the individual, indispensable for seeing new options and constructs to create a moral perspective for himself/herself. It seems to me that this learning process is essential unless we wish to see a new morality, faceless and characterless, emerge as the religious teaching of the public school system.

III The Problem of Relativism

Competing philosophical and psychological models of moral growth, ethical decision-making and affective life bring us directly to the large problem of relativity, relativism, and pluralism in values/moral education, expressed earlier in Justice Brennan's articulation of the paradox of the "rights of conscience," and in Kohlberg's rejection of "the bag of virtues" approach to moral education. (A corollary of this controversy is the relation among religion-studies, religion, faith, morality, and morals/values education and ethics.) To the problem of relativity, relativism and pluralism I quote Professor Scriven, who has articulated the dilemma most accurately:

The confusion of <u>pluralism</u>, of the proper
tolerance for diversity of ideas, with
<u>relativism</u>--the doctrine that there are no
right and wrong answers in ethics or religion--
is perhaps the most serious ideological barrier
to the implementation of moral education today.
The dilemma seems simple: Either we teach a
specific set of moral tenets--in which case we
reject the views of others and hence (apparently)
pluralism--or we teach "empty ethics" ("be good
and avoid evil"), which we well know to be a
waste of time. There is of course a third path:
teaching how to do moral analysis from any given
basis, teaching various views of ethics and
within ethics, and then letting the chips fall
where they may. Values educators, like science
educators, have rightly stressed this
possibility. They have been less careful in
avoiding the attractions of relativism when
doing the process route. It is morally and
pedagogically correct to teach <u>about</u> ethics,
and the <u>skills</u> of moral analysis rather than
doctrine, and to set out arguments for and
against tolerance and pluralism. All of this
is undone if you also imply that all the various
incompatible views about abortion or pornography
or war are equally right, or likely to be right,
or deserving of respect. Pluralism requires
respecting the right to <u>hold</u> divergent beliefs:
it implies <u>neither</u> tolerance of <u>actions</u> based
on those beliefs <u>nor</u> respecting the <u>content</u> of
the beliefs. Some actions are morally
indefensible, even if done "in conscience"--that
is, because dictated by our beliefs (e.g.,
sacrificing one's children to one's gods);
and some beliefs are false, even if we
respect the right of people to hold them
(e.g., the belief that there is a supreme
being who requires the sacrificial killing
of his followers' children). There is an
objectivity of fact--not a perfect
objectivity of knowledge--on which ethics
must be built, or rot away. It does not
justify intolerance, but neither does it
justify relativism or a moral education
that teaches relativism or implies it.[38]

Professor Kohlberg is equally concerned about
relativity, <u>and</u> its opposite, indoctrination. He claims
that "cop-out solutions" to the relativity problem consist
of 1) the hidden curriculum or the "socialization process
of the teacher"; 2) a positive moral and spiritual
approval to value raising the problem of the issue of
which values and why; 3) the bag of virtues approach,
alluded to earlier, describing personality traits in
terms of action; 4) value clarification including
inculcation of openness.[39] Equally, "Religious values
seem to go through the same stages as all other values."[40]

This statement, as the whole tone of Kohlberg's approach, does not relate to content, nor does it relate to the distinctions among moral training, ethical analysis and moral education. Moral training, says Professor Kurt Baier, is associated with the acquired morality of the community.[41] Moral education, on the other hand, consists of teaching by professionals, i.e. philosophers, toward moral excellence.[42]

> What, then, is it for someone to have reached
> the status of a moral being? We should call
> someone a moral being, if he has acquired
> the disposition to do what is morally required
> of him because he knows or thinks it is so
> required. To have this complex disposition,
> he must have three distinguishable but
> connected excellences, the knowledge of
> what is morally required of him, the ability
> to do whatever is morally required of him,
> and the willingness to do whatever he knows
> or thinks is so required.[43]

However, Professor Baier rightly points out that in order to clarify the nature of ethical pluralism one must distinguish among 1) ethical pluralism and ethical diversity;[44] 2) private morality and public morality;[45] 3) legal sanctions and moral sanctions;[46] 4) the principle of tolerance amid a communal education of "good will" toward a public moral order established by the principles of distributing justice. Ethical pluralism then revolves about the question of diversity in unity - the tolerance of private moral dispositions provided the public order is nurtured.[47] It appears to me that relativity is a fact of life; relativism is a distortion of what relativity qua pluralism--thus tolerance--is. Here the sociologist adds to the discussion, justifying a cultural approach to moral/values education.[48]

IV   Moral/Values Education and Religion-Studies

The issue of "Relativity and/or Pluralism" is extremely pertinent to the relationship and distinction between morals/values education and religion-studies. For educationally sound religion-studies world moral pluralism is emphatically required. To do otherwise would be indoctrination. However, the appropriate methodology is unquestionably the issue.[49] I agree with Professor Baier that "empty ethics" is not useful or appropriate. However, I am sure that the art of rational thinking compiled with ethical options may produce reflective individuals--the goal of education.

Insuring that any particular morality will be the public vehicle for moral instruction, and, at the same time, assuring educators of the value of the plural _forms_ of world positions allows individual, _free choice_ in the true sense of the word. Even a country such as Great Britain committed to a "cultural Christianity" is able to recognize the distinction between religious perception and moral perception and between moral knowledge as autonomous and morality as derived from religion. "Likewise, many whose interest is moral education recognize that the insights and accumulated wisdom of the great world religions cannot be ignored in any comprehensive scheme of moral education."[50] What is suggested is a comparative study of morals.[51] While I find the word "comparative" difficult, I would argue for the cross-religious, cross-cultural study of morals. Education would then be teaching <u>about</u> peoples moral perspectives, rather than evaluating what is an "American morality" in the disguise of moral education or religious education.

Because of the confusion of the relationship between what is seen erroneously as a similar purpose served by both moral education and religion-studies, each is viewed as co-equal in objective and intention. While some of the paradoxical problems are shared and even derived from similar sources such as the Supreme Court cases, moral education and religion-studies are distinct enterprises. Morality viewed as ethics, is indeed part of religion-studies, just as moral education contains elements of substance derived from religious perspectives. Yet to haphazardly mix the two disciplines by means of a soft eclecticism would be disastrous. In any approach to the academic study of religion in public schools certain criteria must obtain if it is to be operationally sound. 1) Respect for plural religious forms must be maintained even in teaching what <u>appears</u> common to all. The fact of the matter is that a common morality is <u>not</u> to be found. Diverse religious paradigms may contraindicate what is popularly acceptable as "American Morality." 2) A commitment to the educational process with a primary focus on the health and wholeness of the individual student must be the major concern of any technique or theory. 3) A realistic presentation of the problems of the individual and the group, the individual and society, the group and society, the society and the nation, the nation and the world, must confront both the contradicting truths of life, religion and/or the paradoxes implied in multiple dimensions of human life. When the educational process fails to address these three concerns it is not fulfilling the mandate of the future direction of students as adults in that same world. In the past, great caution has been exercised in the approach to any subject matter termed "religion" or described as "religious." Unfortunately the same caution has not been exercised with respect to science and/or ethical and moral problems. We deem it sufficient to present <u>one</u> approach rather than teach <u>about</u> morality from both the moral education perspective as well as in the context of religion-studies. For example, for science we settle on either evolution or creation: for morality, we adapt values clarification or Kohlberg's moral development. It seems to me that this is a reduction of the issue and its possible responses--a reduction we cannot afford. For we then replace one form of absolute dogmatism with another, chosen for the convenience it provides for filling a mandate, rather than because it satisfies formal criteria for sound pedagogy and appropriate methodology.

V Co-ordinated Efforts: A Proposal

Finally, I would like to suggest a methodological framework for the treatment of the relationship between disciplines, such as religion and science, and religion and ethical problems, which provides a historical context with roots in religious paradigms and the interaction of religion with specific issues. Whether it be alternatives to creation/evolution, diverse moral perspectives or bioethical issues such as abortion, fetal life, death, etc., there exist different world views which provide "plural forms of morality" for the student as he or she truly chooses (decides) to accept a way of looking at these issues for himself/herself. However, as Hall and Davis suggest, a student must know the skills of an inquiry into the nature of the moral before paradigms may speak to the student. The "ethician," or one who is educationally skilled in presenting paradigms of moral behavior in an impartial manner, draws on a plurality of "perspectives" or "moral dispositions" as the student is challenged by a new problem and/or issue. The ethician is able to communicate how paradigms live and operate for the individual, for the society and for civilizational development. The limitations of such paradigms are also demonstrated. Paradigms-of-Reality-in-Process, as I have termed the content of a methodology for the study of problematic areas in public education religion-studies, inaugurate a mean between method as technique and methodology as the form for public school religion-studies.[52]

Likewise moral/values education must evoke a common core of working assumptions so that education and school administration are clear about the diversity of methods existing in the field. The following assumptions are suggested with the intention of A) acknowledging that diversity; B) showing the relationship where appropriate to religion-studies:

1. Schools should adopt a rationale justifying and authorizing teaching about values as distinct from teaching values.[53] "It is perfectly possible to have moral education without reference to religious positions or presuppositions."[54]

2. The rationale should a) acknowledge the diversity of ideologies, schools of thought and methods for morals/values education, including humanist, atheist, etc.; b) recognize that very diverse forms of justification are given for values. (This justification is frequently based on "private beliefs" as well as publicly accepted ones);[55] c) insure against the arbitrary adoption of moral principles and methods.

3. Schools must recognize that plural religious world systems and behaviors are operative in the private beliefs of persons as well as in the public domain.[56]

4. Schools should beware of linking morals too closely with any religious viewpoint, except when it is naturally part of a specific religious tradition or history, e.g. _ahimsa_ (non-injury), non-violence, love, charity.[57]

5. Moral codes may not be extracted from a religion

without learning the history, context, etc. If taught
they (moral codes) must be discussed as paradigms of
religion in life taught as part of a total religion-
studies course.[58]

6. Philosophical and psychological approaches to,
and descriptions of, morals/values must be evaluated
relative to the task of the classroom student and the
merit of the selected approach.[59]

These assumptions accomplish two things: 1) the
distinction between moral education and values inculcation
as well as among moral education, vlaues evaluation and
morality as part of a total religion-studies curriculum;
2) the preconditions for guidelines articulating
competency areas and objectives in both disciplines.

Our four opening questions seem to draw responses
from many corners. While the debt seems to be to Immanuel
Kant for the "why" of moral/values education, the
content and the style of that education vary from the
structured response to the situational, from the specific
values approach to the paradigmatic approach. The core
issue of the paradox of the rights of conscience and the
evaluation of any are moral perspectives seem to be
respected by all. Yet, a value-free methodology of
morals is one thing to theorize about and another to
practice inside the legal public domain. What remains
totally open is further effort to articulate the domain
of the moral and to discover effective moral education
which avoids teaching relativism. Contrary to opinion,
as close as Kohlberg's "school as a just community" comes
to a "religious ideal," it too articulates a moral policy
which confronts our paradox most openly. Professor John
Stewart describes the rationale of the philosophy of
the environment for moral education:

> Kohlberg's derivation of the notion of the
> just community comes primarily from his
> recognition of the fact that only democratic
> environments provide enough opportunity for
> experiencing the very things that promote
> development, e.g., opportunities for
> role-taking, constructive cognitive
> conflict resulting from the encouragement
> of logical thinking, direct individual
> responsibility for making moral decisions,
> influencing one's immediate world through
> direct involvement, exposure to conflict
> in moral reasoning (not just emotional
> conflict) by having one's views challenged
> by people at stages higher than one's own,
> and prolonged exposure to an environment
> that promotes justice.[60]

It appears then that the question of a "value-free
methodology of morals" is set within the important
question of whom we are addressing by moral education.
If one's intention is to create a reality-centered
individual then our task is clear in its content. Yet
the methodology may of itself carry a "hidden curriculum"
unless one directs attention to the art of reflective

thought about morality itself as a primary step to
moral/values education. The key is education. A word
of caution is expressed by John Wilson:

> Much of the trouble here stems from the idea
> that "education" is a sort of pipe-line for
> parental or social values: that being
> educated is a matter of being inculcated
> with certain particular values that we, or
> society, or whatever, happen to like
> ("democracy," for instance). Clearly this
> is rubbish: 'being educated' does not mean
> being inculcated with anything except
> certain kinds of rationality and
> understanding, which are not tied to
> particular cultures or societies. We have
> to see education values as in this respect
> exactly like education in mathematics or
> science or history or any other sphere of
> thought and action. Until we can do this
> and be clearer in detail about it, we cannot
> even seriously start. Anyone who thought
> that "value education" had much to do with
> "society," "the modern world," etc., would
> not, in my view, be seriously interested in
> educating pupils at all, but rather in
> selling some line.[61]

Religion-studies, then, is related to moral education
in that both require a pedagogy of pluralistic
non-indoctrination. Both take as their primary focus
the education of the student toward reflective
understanding of themselves and others in the light of
ways of believing and behaving. But each is a distinct
discipline in that one is not derived from the other.
Religion-studies has a substantive content which includes,
though not exclusively, the academic study of the ethics
of each religion or way of life, in relation to the
religion under study. Moral/values education, on the
other hand, has the express purpose of teaching that
there is, if not a "right" and "wrong" mode of conduct,
at least adequate as opposed to inadequate ways of
reflection and action. While I believe that moral/values
education can be done without indoctrination it would be
safe to conclude that the original intention of moral
education, as suggested by the Supreme Court cases Pierce
vs. the Society of Sisters and Lemon vs. Kurtzman,
indicates that non-indoctrination may not be the
authentic aim of its legal initiators.

Notes

[1] Abington v. Schempp/Murray v. Curtlett, 1963; Calvary Bible Presbyterian Church v. the Board of Regents.

[2] See Pierce v. Society of Sisters, 1925, and Lemon v. Kurtzman, 1971.

[3] Sam Duker, THE PUBLIC SCHOOLS AND RELIGION: The Legal Context. (New York: Harper and Row, 1966), pp. 189-190. A recent statement by the Catholic Bishops of Pennsylvania raises the issue by rebuking public education for both the objective tendency of religion and the teaching of a secularistic morality. (See PUBLIC EDUCATION AND STUDENT CONSCIENCE, Harrisburg, 1976.) While I do not agree with their response to the issue of the rights of conscience I do acknowledge the problem raised. (Note: the Bishops erroneously, however, refer to the McCollum case as prohibiting released-time. This case prohibited dismissed time, [pp. 24-25] or released-time as operating in the Champagne School District.)

[4] Thayer S. Warshaw, RELIGION, PUBLIC EDUCATION AND THE SUPREME COURT, Revised ed. (Indiana University: Institute on the Bible, 1974), p. 25. The passages cited reflect alterations in the 1974 edition communicated in a letter to me by Mr. Warshaw, dated March 6, 1976.

[5] United States v. Seegar, 1965. The Universal Military Training and Service Act of 1948 [Section 6 j] restricted such exemptions to a person "who, by reason of religious training and belief is conscientiously opposed to participation in war in any form...'Religious training and belief' in this connection means an individual's belief in a relation to a Supreme Being involving duties superior to those arising from any human relation but not including essentially political, sociological, or philosophical views or a merely personal moral code."

[6] Ibid., pp. 7-8; cf. U.S. v. Seegar, 1965, p. 21. See the paradox in MORAL AND SPIRITUAL VALUES IN THE PUBLIC SCHOOLS. (Washington, D.C.: National Education Association [Educational Policies Commission], 1951). See also Barnette, 1943.

[7] MORAL EDUCATION: Interdisciplinary Approaches. (New York: Newman Press, 1971), p. 21.

[8] Cf. Lawrence Kohlberg, "Education for Justice; a Modern Statement of the Platonic View," in MORAL EDUCATION: 5 Lectures, With an Introduction by Nancy F. and Theodore R. Sizer. (Cambridge: Harvard University Press, 1970), p. 63; cf. Kohlberg, "Indoctrination versus Relativity in Value Education," ZYGON VI, #4, Dec. 1971, pp. 285-310.

[9] Ibid., p. 67. More recently Kohlberg has adopted a philosophy of "the school as a just community." See note 22.

[10] Ibid., pp. 69-70.

[11] Cf. Kohlberg, "Stages of Moral Development as a Basis for Moral Education,' in MORAL EDUCATION: Interdisciplinary Approaches, op. cit., pp. 36-38. Cf. Kohlberg, "Moral Education, Religious Education, and the Public Schools: A Developmental View," in RELIGION AND PUBLIC EDUCATION. Edited by Theodore Sizer, (Boston: Houghton Mifflin, 1967), p. 179 as quoted by Oliver and Bane, op. cit., p. 259: "A definition of the aim of moral education as the stimulation of natural development appears, then, to be clear-cut in the area of moral judgment, which has considerable regularity of sequences and direction in development in various cultures. Because of this regularity, it is possible to define the maturity of a child's moral judgment without considering its content (the particular action judged) and without considering whether or not it agrees with our own particular moral judgments or values or those of the American middle-class culture as a whole. In fact, the sign of the child's moral maturity is his ability to make moral judgments and formulate moral principles of his own, rather than his ability to conform to moral judgments of the adults around him."

[12] Ibid., pp. 38-39.

[13] Ibid., p. 39.

[14] Richard S. Peters, "A Reply to Kohlberg," in KAPPAN LVI, #10, June, 1975, p. 678. See also D.C. Phillips and Mavis E. Kelly, "Hierarchical Theories of Development in Education and Psychology," HARVARD EDUCATIONAL REVIEW XLV, #3, August, 1975, pp. 351-375. "The authors examine the much-touted hierarchical theories of development and argue that their underlying assumptions have not been adequately examined. One special concern is the claim that the order of stages of development must be invariant; another is the problem of clarifying the contribution that earlier stages make to succeeding stages...(from Opening Abstract).

[15] Ibid., cf. Part 2 of Richard S. Peters (ed.), PSYCHOLOGY AND ETHICAL DEVELOPMENT, (London: Allen and Unwin, 1974); "Moral Development: A Plea for Pluralism," in Theodore Mischel, COGNITIVE DEVELOPMENT AND EPISTEMOLOGY, (New York: Academic Press, 1971) and "Moral Education and the Psychology of Character" in Richard S. Peters, PSYCHOLOGY AND ETHICAL DEVELOPMENT, op. cit.

[16] Ibid.

[17] Kenneth Keniston, THE UNCOMMITTED: Alienated Youth in American Society, (Dell Publishing Co. [A Delta Book], 1965 [1960]).

[18] Kenneth Keniston, "Youth and Violence: The Contexts [49.] of Moral Crisis," in MORAL EDUCATION: 5 Lectures op. cit., pp. 109-110. Cf. YOUNG RADICALS, (New York: Harcourt, Brace and World, 1968).

[19] Donald W. Oliver and M.J. Bane, "Moral Education: Is Reasoning Enough?", in MORAL EDUCATION: Interdisciplinary Approaches, op. cit., p. 253.

[20] Ibid.; cf. Donald W. Oliver, Fred M. Newmann, and Mary Jo Bane, Public Issues Series: CASES AND CONTROVERSY, (American Education Publications, 1967).

[21] Cf. S.I. Benn and R.S. Peters, The Principles of Political Thought, (New York: The Free Press, 1959), p. 63, as quoted by Oliver and Bane, op. cit. p. 258: Our own view of moral education clearly focuses on moral reasoning, and is more in line with the conclusions expressed by Benn and Peters: Our view about morality, therefore, which we have expounded by considering the contributions of the main schools of moral theory can be summed up as follows:
i A moral rule differs from a customary one in that it implies the autonomy of the individual. A rule becomes moral by by being critically accepted by the individual in the light of certain criteria.
ii The criteria can be summarized by saying that the rule should be considered in the light of the needs and interests of people likely to be affected by it with no partiality towards the claims of any of those whose needs and interests are at stake.
iii The acceptance of such criteria is implied, albeit in a minimal degree, by the notion of rationality in the sense of reasonableness.
Our contention is, therefore, that there is a sense in which moral philosophy or ethics, which is the attempt to make explicit the criteria in terms of which rules are morally justified, itself exemplifies, in a minimum degree, the acceptance of the criteria which it attempts to make explicit.

[22] Oliver and Bane, op. cit., p. 261. See also note 9. Kohlberg has shifted toward the motivations of the classroom as a "just community," resembling their theoretical framework but utilizing the democratic community orientation toward the teaching of justice. For a review of this position see John S. Stewart, "The School as a Just Community: Transactional-Developmental Moral Education," in VALUES EDUCATION: Theory/Practice/Problems/Prospects. Edited by John R. Meyer, Brian Burnham and John Cholvat. (Waterloo, Ontario, Canada: Wilfrid Laurier University Press, 1975), pp. 149-162.

[23] Ibid., pp. 264-265.

[24] Sidney Selig and Gerald Teller, "The Moral Development of Children in Three Different School Settings,"

RELIGIOUS EDUCATION LXX, #4, July/August 1975, p. 414.
I would also recommend Janice Sam's article, "The
Ghetto Child and Moral Development," RELIGIOUS
EDUCATION LXX, #6, Nov./Dec., 1975, pp. 636-648. "One
of the major criticisms I have expressed...concerns
this very universality as it applies particularly to
the ghetto child as he/she develops morality within
that culture" (p. 636). See also VALUES EDUCATION:...,
op. cit., pp. 149-162. See also Justin Aronfreed,
"Some Problems for a Theory of the Acquisition of
Conscience," in MORAL EDUCATION: Interdisciplinary
Approaches, op. cit., pp. 183-199. "The placement of
a potential act on a cognitive dimension or standard
of conscience does not in itself give an assignment of
value. Values have certain irreducible affective
components. It is the nature and strength of these
affective components, and not merely the cognitive
substance of values, that permit the values to
exercise control over overt behaviour" (p. 190).
Aronfreed's thesis reflects the problem of "the place
of moral values in the broader arena of socialization,
on the consideration of how any type of evaluative
scheme (regardless of its moral status) might require
control over the child's conduct, and on the
requirements for a more general conception of the
acquisition of values" (p. 185). See also David E.
Hunt, "Matching Models and Moral Training," MORAL
EDUCATION, op. cit., pp. 231-251.

25 See Michel Scriven's article, "Cognitive Moral
Education," KAPPAN, op. cit., pp. 689-694, for one
perspective. See also Brian Crittenden, "A Comment
on Cognitive Moral Education," ibid., pp. 695-696, for
an opposing viewpoint.

26 Cf. Sidney B. Simon, Leland W. Howe, Howard Kirshenbaum,
VALUES CLARIFICATION: A Handbook of Practical
Strategies for Teachers and Students. (New York: Hart
Publishing Company, 1972); Louis E. Raths, Merill Harmin,
Sidney B. Simon, VALUES AND TEACHING, (Columbus:
Charles E. Merrill and Company, 1966).

27 See John R. Meyer, ASPECTS AND MODELS OF VALUES/MORAL
EDUCATION. (Burlington, Ontario: Values Education
Centre, 1975), p. 1: "The assumption is that a person
can have some control over his or her destiny. Thus the
essential behavior of a 'moral agent' is characterized
by:
1. autonomy and responsibility for the efforts of
one's actions;
2. identification and expression of self-held
values (dignity and worth);
3. formulation of action proposals consistent with
his or her values;
4. recognition of the valuing of others and projection
of the consequences of his or her action proposals
for others;
5. selection of actions which most effectively serve
self-held values and do not contradict the valuing

of others;

6. consistent action of stated values;
7. evaluation of the effects on self and others.
Our program seeks to promote the growth of learners
as thinking and feeling persons whose judgments will
be grounded on factual analysis and sound reasoning
while tempered with empathy and compassion for others.
This is, in turn, premised on the assumption that
educators and their institutions have the task of
assisting learners in their quest for a clear,
consistent, and defensible system of values."
See also, Pilot Project in "Affective Education through
Values Education," Ministry of Concept for Affective
Education," in Values Colloquium IV, THE EDUCATIONAL
SITUATION AS A MILIEU FOR MATURING. Sponsored by The
Religion in Education Foundation May 14-17, 1970,
Santa Barbara, California, pp. 71-83.

[28] Robert T. Hall and John U. Davis, MORAL EDUCATION IN
THEORY AND PRACTICE, (New York: Prometheus Books, 1975).
See John Wilson, Norman Williams, Barry Sugarman,
INTRODUCTION TO MORAL EDUCATION, (New York: Penguin
Books, 1967).

[29] Michael Scriven, "Cognitive Moral Education," in KAPPAN,
op. cit., p. 690.

[30] Ibid.

[31] Louis E. Raths et al., VALUES AND TEACHING, op. cit.,
pp. 35-36.

[32] Ibid., p. 30.

[33] See the strategies in VALUES CLARIFICATION: A Handbook
..., op. cit.

[34] Hall and Davis, op. cit., p. 46. See also John Wilson,
"How to Study 'Value Education," in VALUES EDUCATION:...,
op. cit., pp. 165-167.

[35] Ibid., p. 38.

[36] Ibid., p. 38.

[37] Ibid., p. 65.

[38] Scriven, op. cit., p. 694. The Cognitive Curriculum
(pp. 692-693) includes: 1) knowledge about and
understanding of the facts, including arguments and
positions, involved in moral issues; 2) the cognitive
skills of moral reasoning, developed to the level...
where they can be exercised in social argumentation...;
3) the nature, origin, and foundation of ethics...
including such questions as, What is it that
distinguishes morality from convention, orders,
self-interest, etc.? (meta-ethics).

[39] Lawrence Kohlberg, "Indoctrination versus Relativity

in Values Education, op cit., pp. 286-290. Cf. note
10 re: values clarification and value inculcation in
P. Engel, unpublished address, as quoted in Sidney
Simon, "Value-Clarification vs. Indoctrination,"
SOCIAL EDUCATION XXXV, 1971, p. 902.

[40] Kohlberg, ibid., p. 303.

[41] Cf. Kurt Baier, "ethical Pluralism and Moral Education,"
in MORAL EDUCATION: Interdisciplinary Approaches, op.
cit., pp. 93-95.

[42] Baier defines moral education as "a deliberate activity,
carried on previously by professional teachers, for the
purpose of fostering moral excellence in the young."
"Moral excellence" is, in my judgment, a vague and mis-
leading description of what constitutes excellence since
"moral excellence" is an empty ethic. See pp. 95-96.

[43] Ibid., p. 96. In contrast to Baier's description,
Kenneth Keniston defines morals and ethics respectively;
Morals are "socially learned, largely unconscious,
relatively specific and apparently self-evident rules
of right conduct in any community. When an individual
violates his moral code, he feels guilt, the pangs of
conscience experienced as a part of the 'not-me', as an
alien force that acts upon the conscious in experiencing
self." Ethics is "an individual's thought-out,
reflective and generalized sense of good and evil, the
desirable and the undesirable as integrated into his
sense of himself and his view of the world. When an
ethical man violates his own ethics, he feels not guilt
but a sense of being a failure, a kind of extential
shame that he has not been who he thought himself to be.
A man's conscience is commonly experienced as alien;
but his ethical sense is a part (often the heart) of
his central and best self. Moral codes tend to be
specific and situational; but ethical principles are
generally universal, seeking to provide guidelines for
conduct in all possible situations. While morals tell
us how to behave, ethics tells us what to aspire to.
Therefore the central conflict of the moral life is the
struggle between instincts and morals; but the central
tension of the ethical life is the question of how to
achieve one's ethical aims." See "Morals and Ethics,"
THE AMERICAN SCHOLAR XXXIV, Autumn, 1965, pp. 628-634.

[44] Cf. Ibid., pp. 101f. "What differentiates ethical
pluralism from mere ethical diversity is the fact
that the activities regulated by these different moral
convictions are co-operative or competitive and
therefore impinge on the lives of those engaging in
them, which is not so in cases of mere ethical
diversity. The main problem created by ethical
pluralism therefore arises even when the groups while
opposing moralities are not parts of a social or
political whole, such as a multi-nation state or a
state comprising a great many ethnically diverse
groups as long as they do not live in conditions of

total apartheid."   53.

[45] Ibid., p. 103. See also, Barbara Ann DeMartin Swyhart,
BIOETHICAL DECISION-MAKING: Releasing Religion from
the Spiritual, (Philadelphia: Fortress Press, 1975),
"The Emerging Ethician."

[46] Ibid., p. 105.

[47] Ibid., pp. 108-112. This position is apparently the
guiding one in the coverage of the concept of
"Morality" as expressed in the work study proposal,
"Social Science Topic and Content: Preamble," (1975)
as prepared for consideration by the state of
California: "Every society, as part of the process of
socialization, inculcates in the child a set of values
and a code of relevant standards for behavioral
responses. Value systems and their relationship to
alternative patterns of social organization and human
institutions are examined in social sciences and again
are vital materials in cross-cultural appraisals.
Particular values and codes shift with cultural context,
but in all cases there is general acceptance of a
morality which is seen by the culture to be an integral
part of its definition. Many of the most basic values
appear to be universal but are ranked in differing
hierarchies. Those aspects of values and codes which
are not universal serve to unite the individual with
his own groupings and separate him from those of which
he is not a part. Questions should deal with the
processes and agent of moral teaching, with the
universal aspects of morality across cultures, with an
appreciation of cultural differences in values, and
with the candidate's understanding of the worth of
systems other than the candidate's own."

[48] Cf. J. Theodore Klein, "Cultural Pluralism and Moral
Education," in THE MONIST LVIII, #4, October, 1974,
pp. 683-693; Thomas F. Green, EDUCATION AND PLURALISM:
Ideal and Reality, (Syracuse, New York: School of
Education, Syracuse University, 1966); Seymour W.
Itzkoff, CULTURAL PLURALISM AND AMERICAN EDUCATION,
(Scranton, Pennsylvania: International Textbook Co.,
1969).

[49] Michael Scriven in "Cognitive Moral Education," op. cit.,
p. 693 suggests that we "tippy-toe" around the issues of
the role of conscience and the contributions of Buddha,
Mohammed, Confucius, the prophets, etc. to moral
pluralism (my term).

[50] RELIGIOUS EDUCATION IN SECONDARY SCHOOLS, Schools
Council Working Paper 36, (London: Evans/Mcthuen
Educational, Ltd., 1971), especially, "Religious
Education and Moral Education," p. 69.

[51] Ibid., p. 70. See James Smurl, RELIGIOUS ETHICS: A
Systems Approach, (New Jersey: Prentice Hall, 1972).

[52] Adapted from Swyhart, "Paradigms-of-Reality-in-Process: A Methodology for Interdisciplinary Religion-Studies," to be published in RELIGIOUS EDUCATION, 1976. The first draft was presented at the American Academy of Religion, October 1975, and appeared as "Public Education Religion-Studies: Toward an Operational Process Methodology for Science, Religion and Ethics," in THE ACADEMIC STUDY OF RELIGION, 1975. Compiled by Anne Carr and Nicholas Piediscalzi, Scholars Press, 1975. This framework is part of a book in preparation, AN EMERGING PROFESSION: Academic Religion-Studies in Public Education.

[53] Adapted from Paul H. Hirst, "Public and Private Values and Religious Educational Content," in Theodore R. Sizer (ed.), RELIGION AND PUBLIC EDUCATION, (Boston: Houghton Mifflin Company, 1967), pp. 329-339.

[54] Taken from the Schools Council Working Paper 36, RELIGIOUS EDUCATION IN SECONDARY SCHOOLS, London: Evans/Mcthuen Educational Ltd., 1971, p. 70.

[55] Ibid. Changes are my own. Other publicly accepted traditions include humanist, secular, ethical culturist, atheist, etc., so defined as "religious" equivalents in legal terms in Torcaso vs. Watkins, 1970.

[56] The Schools Council Working Paper 36, op. cit., p. 70.

[57] Ibid. Adaptation is my own.

[58] Cf. Swyhart, op. cit.

[59] Reflected in the purpose of this paper.

[60] John S. Stewart, "The School as a Just Community...," op. cit., p. 150. See also L. Kohlberg, K. Kaufmann, P. Scharf, J. Hickey, THE JUST COMMUNITY APPROACH TO CORRECTIONS: A Manual, Part I and II (Cambridge: Moral Education Research Foundation, Harvard University), 1974.

[61] John Wilson, "How to Study 'Value Education'," in VALUES EDUCATION: Theory/Practice/Problems/Prospects, op. cit., p. 167.

Selected Bibliography on Moral Education,
Values Clarification, and Moral Development,
in Relation to Religion-Studies

Allen, Rodney F., TEACHING GUIDE TO THE PLOVER BOOKS,
     Terrace Heights: St. Mary's College Press (Plover
     Books Series), 1974.

THE AMERICAN SCHOLAR, "A Symposium on Morality." Summer,
     1965, pp. 336-347; "On Morality: Comments on the
     Scholars' Symposium," Fall, 1965, pp. 620-636.

Aristotle, NICHOMACHEAN ETHICS. Translated by J.A.
     Thompson. New York: Penguin Books, 1953.

Aronfreed, Justin, "Some Problems for a Theory of the
     Acquisition of Conscience," pp. 183-199 in MORAL
     EDUCATION: Interdisciplinary Approaches, ed. by
     Beck, et al. (see entry).

Ausubel, David P., "Psychology's Underevaluation of the
     Rational Components in Moral Behavior," pp. 200-227
     in MORAL EDUCATION: Interdisciplinary Approaches
     (see entry).

Baier, Kurt, "Ethical Pluralism and Moral Education,"
     pp. 93-112 in MORAL EDUCATION: Interdisciplinary
     Approaches (see entry).

Baier, Kurt, "Moral Development," pp. 601-615 in THE
     MONIST (see entry).

Barbour, Ian G., MYTHS, MODELS AND PARADIGMS. New York:
     Harper and Row, 1974.

Beck, Clive, "Moral Education in the Schools: Some
     Practical Suggestions" PROFILES FOR PRACTICAL
     EDUCATION No. 3; Toronto: Ontario Institute for
     Studies in Education (OISE), 1971.

Beck, Clive; Crittenden, B.S.; Sullivan, E.V. (eds.),
     MORAL EDUCATION: Interdisciplinary Approaches.
     New York: Newman Press, 1971.

Benn, S.I., and Peters, R.S., THE PRINCIPLES OF POLITICAL
     THOUGHT. New York: The Free Press, 1959.

Benson, George C.S. (with Dr. T.S. Engeman), "Practical
     Possibilities in American Moral Education,"
     JOURNAL OF MORAL EDUCATION IV, 31, October, 1974,
     pp. 53-66.

BIBLIOGRAPHY IN MORAL/VALUES EDUCATION, 3rd ed., The
     Association of Values Education Resources,
     University of British Columbia Computing Centre,
     1975. Write to Dr. William Bruneau, A.V.E.R.
     Faculty of Education, University of British
     Columbia, Vancouver, B.C. Canada $20.).

Bettelheim, Bruno, "Moral Education," pp. 85-107 in MORAL
    EDUCATION: 5 Lectures (see entry).

Black, Max, MODELS AND METAPHORS. Ithaca, New York:
    Cornell University Press, 1962.

Blatt, Moshe M., and Kohnberg, L., "The Effects of
    Classroom Moral Discussion upon Children's Level of
    Moral Judgment," JOURNAL OF MORAL EDUCATION IV, #2,
    February, 1975.

Bruner, Jerome, THE PROCESS OF EDUCATION. New York:
    Vintage Books, 1953.

Bruner, Jerome, THE RELEVANCE OF EDUCATION. Edited by
    Anita Gil. New York: W. W. Norton, 1971.

Burch, Robert W., "Are there Moral Experts?", pp. 646-
    658 in THE MONIST (see entry).

Burnham, Brian, "Human Values Education: The New Dynamic
    in Program Development," EDUCATION CANADA XV, 1,
    Spring, 1975, pp. 4-10.

Burns, George, and Hall, Robert T., "Moral Awareness in
    Psychological Testing and Experimentation," Moral
    Education Development Project, Grant from NEH,
    1975, College of Steubenville, Steubenville, Ohio.

Buss, Virginia, and McFarland, George, "Simulation Gaming
    and Religious Education," A special theme section
    in SIMULATION/GAMING/NEWS, March, 1974, pp. 6-13.

California State Board of Education, HANDBOOK ON THE LEGAL
    RIGHTS AND RESPONSIBILITIES OF SCHOOL PERSONNEL AND
    STUDENTS IN THE AREAS OF MORAL AND CIVIC EDUCATION
    AND TEACHING ABOUT RELIGION. Sacramento: The
    California Board of Education, 1973.

Carey, Maureen; Chapman, Paul; Cunnane, Robert; Mullaney,
    Antony; Walsh, Anne, DECIDING ON THE HUMAN USE OF
    POWER: The Exercise and Control of Power in an Age
    of Crisis. Terrace Heights, Winona, Minnesota: St.
    Mary's College Press (Plover Books), 1974.

Catholic Bishops of Pennsylvania, PUBLIC EDUCATION AND
    STUDENT CONSCIENCE: A Dilemma for Concerned
    Citizens. A Statement. Harrisburg: Pennsylvania
    Catholic Conference, February, 1976.

Cochran, Don (ed.), ASSOCIATION NOTES AND RESOURCES IN
    MORAL EDUCATION, The California Association of
    Moral Education.

Connell, William F., "Moral Education: Aims and Methods
    in China, the Ussr and England," KAPPAN, June,
    1975, pp. 702-706.

Connery, Jeremiah W., VALUES IN AN AGE OF CONFRONTATION,

Value Colloquium I & II. Columbus, Ohio: Charles
E. Merrill Publishing Co., 1970.

Cook, Stuart W., "Research Plans in the Fields of
Education, Values and Morality and their Bearing on
Religion-Studies Formation," formulated at The
Research Planning Workshop on Religious Character
Education, Cornell University, August 18-29, 1961;
1962, The Religious Education Association.

Cranor, Carl, "Towards a Theory of Respect for persons,"
AMERICAN PHILOSOPHICAL QUARTERLY XII, #4, October,
1975, pp. 309-319.

Crittenden, Brian, "A Comment on Cognitive Moral
Education," KAPPAN, June, 1975, pp. 695-696.

deTocqueville, Alexis, DEMOCRACY IN AMERICA. Translated
by Henry Reeve Francis, 1962. New York: Alfred A.
Knopf, 1966. Edited with an Introduction by
Phillips Bardley.

Dewey, John, A COMMON FAITH. New Haven: Yale University
Press, 1934 (Yale paperbound, 1964).

Dewey, John, DEMOCRACY AND EDUCATION: An Introduction to
the Philosophy of Education. New York: MacMillan,
1916.

Dewey, John, "Education as Religion," THE NEW REPUBLIC
XXXII, September, 1922, pp. 64-65.

Dewey, John, THE EDUCATIONAL FRONTIER. New York:
Century Company, 1933.

Dewey, John, EXPERIENCE AND EDUCATION. New York:
MacMillan, 1938.

Dewey, John, HUMAN NATURE AND CONDUCT. New York: H.
Holt & Co., 1922, pp. 295-296.

Dewey, John, MORAL PRINCIPLES IN EDUCATION. New York:
Houghton Mifflin Company, 1909.

Dewey, John, MY PEDAGOGIC CREED (1897). Reprinted by the
Progressive Education Association, Washington, D.C.,
1929.

Dewey, John, "Teaching Ethics in High School,"
EDUCATIONAL REVIEW VI, November, 1893, pp. 313-21.

Dodder, Clyde, and Barbara, DECISION-MAKING: A Guide for
Teachers Who Would Help Pre-Adolescent Children
Become Imaginative and Responsible Decision Makers.
Boston: Beacon Press, 1968.

Donnellan, Michael, "Religion and Value Education,"
NATIONAL COUNCIL ON RELIGION AND PUBLIC EDUCATION
II, #1, February, 1975, p. 2.

Durkheim, Émile, PROFESSIONAL ETHICS AND CIVIC MORALS.
    Translated by Cornelia Brookfield. Glencoe, Ill:
    Free Press, 1958.

Elliott, Murray, "The Work of the Assocication for
    Values Education and Research," BULLETIN, Canadian
    Society for the Study of Education, (Box 1000,
    Faculty of Education, University of Alberta,
    Edmond, Alberta T6G ZE1) (IV, 2, February, 1975.)

Eisenberg, John, CANADIAN PUBLIC ISSUES PROJECT (booklets),
    The Canadian Critical Issues Series.

Erikson, Erik H., CHILDHOOD AND SOCIETY, 2nd ed. New
    York: W.W. Norton & Co., Inc., 1968.

Erikson, Erik H., IDENTITY, YOUTH AND CRISIS. New York:
    W.W. Norton & Co., Inc., 1968.

Fenton, Edwin (ed.), THE CARNEGIE-MELLON SOCIAL STUDIES
    CURRICULUM (6 vol.), New York: Holt, Rinehart and
    Winston, 1973-75.

Fiske, E.B., "New Techniques Help Pupils Develop Values,"
    NEW YORK TIMES, April 30, 1975.

Freund, Paul A., and Ulrich, Robert, RELIGION AND THE
    PUBLIC SCHOOLS. Cambridge: Harvard University
    Press, 1965.

Galbraith, Ronald E., and Jones, Thomas M., MORAL
    REASONING. Anoka, Minnesota: Greenhaven Press,
    Inc., 1976.

Galbraith, Ronald E., and Jones, Thomas M., "Teaching
    Strategies for Moral Dilemmas," An Application of
    Kohlberg's Theory of Moral Development to the
    Social Studies Classroom," SOCIAL EDUCATION XXXIX,
    1, January, 1975, pp. 16-22.

Gauthier, David P., "Moral Action and Moral Education,"
    pp. 138-146 in MORAL EDUCATION: Interdisciplinary
    Approaches (see entry).

Gustafson, James; Peters, Richard S.; Kohlberg, Lawrence;
    Bettelheim, Bruno; Keniston, Kenneth, MORAL
    EDUCATION: 5 Lectures. With an Introduction by
    Nancy F. and Theodore R. Sizer. Cambridge:
    Harvard University Press, 1970.

Hall, Brian P., THE DEVELOPMENT OF CONSCIOUSNESS: A
    Confluent Theory of Values. Paramus, New Jersey:
    Paulist-Newman Press, 1976.

Hall, Brian P., VALUE CLARIFICATION AS LEARNING PROCESS:
    A Sourcebook for Education. Paramus, New Jersey:
    Paulist-Newman Press, 1974 (Educator Formation
    Books).

Hall, Robert T.,and Davis, John U., MORAL EDUCATION IN
    THEORY AND PRACTICE. New York: Prometheus Books,
    1975.

Hare, R.M., "Rationism in Moral Education: Two Varieties,"
    THE MONIST, pp. 568-580 (see entry).

Harris, William Torrey, "Moral Education, I," AMERICAN
    JOURNAL OF EDUCATION VIII, October, 1875, pp. 4-5.

Harris, William Torrey, "Moral Education, II," AMERICAN
    JOURNAL OF EDUCATION VIII, November, 1875, pp. 4-5.

Harris, William Torrey, "Moral Education, III," AMERICAN
    JOURNAL OF EDUCATION IX, January, 1876.

Harris, William Torrey, "Moral Education in the Common
    School," EDUCATIONAL FOUNDATIONS XIV, October, 1902,
    pp. 68-83.

Harris, William Torrey with Mowry, W.A.; Hoose, J.H.;
    Tarbell, H.S.; and Hall, G.S., "Moral Education in
    Schools--Report of the Committee on Moral
    Education to the National Council of Education,"
    EDUCATION III, 1883.

Harris, William Torrey, "Our Public Schools: Can Morality
    Be Taught Without Sectarianism?," (Symposium)
    JOURNAL OF EDUCATION XXIX, February 14, 1889.

Harris, William Torrey, "Sound Culture in the Form of
    Education Religion," EDUCATIONAL REVIEW XXIX,
    1905, pp. 18-37.

Hartshorne, H., and May, M., STUDIES IN CHARACTER. New
    York: MacMillan, 1928-30.

Hirst, Paul, H., MORAL EDUCATION IN A SECULAR SOCIETY.
    University of London Press, 1975 (University of
    London Press Ltd., St. Paul's House, Warwick Lane,
    London ED4P - 4AH).

Hirst, Paul H., and Peters, R.S., THE LOGIC OF EDUCATION.
    London: Routledge & Kegan Paul, 1970.

Hirst, Paul H., "Public and Private Value and Religious
    Educational Content" in RELIGION AND PUBLIC
    EDUCATION. Edited by Theodore Sizer. Boston:
    Houghton Mifflin, 1967.

THE HISTORY AND SOCIAL SCIENCE TEACHER, Fall, 1975.

Hunt, David E., "Matching Models and Moral Training,"
    pp. 231-251 in MORAL EDUCATION: Interdisciplinary
    Approaches (see entry).

Hunt, David E., and Sullivan, Edward V., BETWEEN
    PSYCHOLGY AND EDUCATION. Hinsdale, Illinois:
    Dryden Press, 1974.

Jones, Hardy E., "The Rationale of Moral Education,"
    pp. 659-673 in THE MONIST (see entry).

JOURNAL OF MORAL EDUCATION, Pemberton Publishing Company,
    Ltd., 88 Islington High Street, London NI - 8EW.

Kant, Immanuel, GROUNDWORK OF A METAPHYSICS OF MORALS.
    Translated and analyzed by H.J. Paton. New York:
    Harper Torchbooks, 1964.

KAPPAN (Phi Delta Kappa) XLVI, #2, October, 1964, Special
    Issue: The Schools and Moral Responsibility.

KAPPAN LVI, #10, June, 1975, Special Issue: Moral
    Education.

Kazepides, A.C., THE TEACHING OF VALUES IN CANADIAN
    EDUCATION, Vol. II, 1975, The Yearbook of the
    Canadian Society for the Study of Education.

Keniston, Kenneth, "Moral Development, Youthful Activism;
    and Modern Society," THE CRITIC XXVIII, September/
    October, 1969, pp. 17-24.

Keniston, Kenneth, "Morals and Ethics," in "On Morality:
    Comments on the Scholar's Symposium, Summer, 1965"
    in THE AMERICAN SCHOLAR XXXIV, Autumn, 1965, pp.
    628-634.

Keniston, Kenneth, THE UNCOMMITTED: Alienated Youth in
    American Society. New York: Dell Publishing Co.,
    Inc., (A Delta Book) [1960] 1965.

Keniston, Kenneth, "Youth and Violence: The Contexts of
    Moral Crisis," pp. 109-131 in MORAL EDUCATION: 5
    Lectures (see entry).

Kirschenbaum, Howard, and Simon, Sidney B., READINGS FOR
    VALUES CLARIFICATION. Minneapolis, Minnesota:
    Winston Press, 1973.

Kirschenbaum, Howard, mimeographed paper, "Recent Research
    in Values Clarification," Upper Jay, New York:
    National Humanistic Education Center, 1974.

Klein, J. Theodore, "Cultural Pluralism and Moral
    Education," pp. 683-693 in THE MONIST (see entry).

Kohlberg, Lawrence, COLLECTED PAPERS ON MORAL DEVELOPMENT
    AND MORAL EDUCATION, I (1973). Moral Education and
    Research Foundation, Roy E. Larson Hill, Harvard
    University.

Kohlberg, Lawrence, "Education for Justice: A Modern
    Statement of the Platonic View," pp. 57-83 in
    MORAL EDUCATION: 5 Lectures (see entry).

Kohlberg, Lawrence, "Education, Moral Development and
    Faith," JOURNAL OF MORAL EDUCATION IV, #1, October,

1974, pp. 5-16 (on stage 7).   61.

Kohlberg, Lawrence, "Indoctrination versus Relativity in
      Value Education," ZYGON, Vol. VI, #4, pp. 285-310.

Kohlberg, Lawrence, "Moral Education," INTERNATIONAL
      ENCYCLOPEDIA OF THE SOCIAL SCIENCES, 1968, pp.
      489-494.

Kohlberg, Lawrence, and Turiel, E., "Moral Development
      and Moral Education," in G. Lesser (ed.),
      PSYCHOLOGY AND EDUCATIONAL PRACTICE, Scott,
      Foresman, 1971.

Kohlberg, Lawrence, "The Child as Moral Philosopher,"
      PSYCHOLOGY TODAY VII, 1968, pp. 25-30.

Kohlberg, Lawrence, "Moralization: The Cognitive-
      Developmental Approach," in Thomas Lickona (ed.),
      MORALITY: Theory, Research and Social Issues.
      New York: Holt, Rinehart, and Winston, 1976.

Kohlberg, Lawrence, "Stages of Moral Development as a
      Basis for Moral Education," MORAL EDUCATION.
      Edited by Beck and Sullivan, Toronto: University
      of Toronto Press, 1970.

Kohlberg, Lawrence, "The Cognitive-Developmental Approach
      to Moral Education" pp. 670-677, in KAPPAN, June,
      1975 (see entry).

Kuhn, Thomas S., THE STRUCTURE OF SCIENTIFIC REVOLUTIONS,
      2nd ed. Chicago: University of Chicago Press,
      1970.

LEARNING FOR LIVING, II, #3, January, 1972, SCM Press Ltd.,
      (56 Bloomsbury Street, London WC1B 3QX $2.00).

LEARNING TO CARE: Teacher's Guide for LIFELINE, Values
      Education Curriculum, LIFELINE, Argus Communications,
      Niles, Illinois.

Lickona, Thomas (ed.), MORAL DEVELOPMENT AND BEHAVIOR:
      Theory, Research and Social Issues. New York:
      Holt, Rinehart, and Winston, 1976. An extensive
      bibliography is given.

Lockwood, Alan L., "A Cultural View of Value
      Clarification," TEACHER'S COLLEGE RECORD LXXVII,
      #1, September, 1975, pp. 35-50.

Lockwood, Alan, MORAL REASONING: The Value of Life.
      Columbus, Ohio: American Education Publications,
      1972.

Lorber, Neil M., "Conformity vs. Nonconformity to Social
      Ethics: The Challenge to Education," pp. 674-682
      in THE MONIST (see entry).

Loubser, Jan. J., "The Contribution of Schools to Moral Development: A Working Paper in the Theory of Action," pp. 147-179 in MORAL EDUCATION: Interdisciplinary Approaches (see entry).

Marks, Ruth, "Moral Education and the Teaching of Values: Resources," ORBIT 26, February, 1975, pp. 16-18.

McClendon, UNDERSTANDING RELIGIOUS CONVICTIONS. Notre Dame: University of Notre Dame Press, 1975.

McClusky, Neil, S.J., PUBLIC SCHOOLS AND MORAL EDUCATION. New York: Greenwood Press, 1975, (1958).

Meldon, A.I., "Moral Education and Moral Action," pp. 115-137 in MORAL EDUCATION: Interdisciplinary Approaches (see entry).

Meyer, John R., ASPECTS AND MODELS OF VALUES/MORAL EDUCATION. Unpublished monograph, Values Education Centre, Burlington, Ontario, Canada, 1974.

Meyer, John R., "Is Values Education Necessary and Justified?" THE SCHOOL GUIDANCE WORKER, November/December, 1975.

Meyer, John R., "Projects and Prospects: Applied Research in Values Education" (Reprint, available from Guidance Center, Faculty of Education, University of Toronto, 1000 Yonge Street, Toronto, Canada M4W 2K8).

Meyer, John R., VALUES EDUCATION: Some Reflections on a Pilot Project in Southern Ontario (Reprint no. 02-335, Guidance Centre, Faculty Education, University of Toronto), reprinted from COMMENT ON EDUCATION V, April, 1975, pp. 15-18.

Meyer, John; Burnham, Brian; Cholvat, John (eds.), VALUES EDUCATION: Theory/Practice/Problems/Prospects. Waterloo: Wilfrid Laurier University Press, 1975.

Michaelson, Robert, PIETY IN THE PUBLIC SCHOOL: Trends and Issues in the Relationship Between Religion and Public School in the United States. The Macmillan Company, 1970. Especially "Common School, Common Faith?".

Mischel, Theodore, COGNITIVE DEVELOPMENT AND EPISTEMOLOGY. New York: Academic Press, 1971.

THE MONIST. A Special Issue: "The Philosophy of Moral Education" XLVIII, #4, October, 1974.

"Moral Education," NEWSWEEK, March 1, 1976, pp. 74-75A.

MORAL EDUCATION CONSORTIUM NEWSLETTER (Dr. Lisa Kuhmerker, 221 East 72nd Street, New York, NY 10021).

"Morals and Spiritual Education in Kentucky," DEPARTMENT
    OF EDUCATION XXVI, #1, January, 1958.

MORAL AND SPIRITUAL VALUES IN PUBLIC EDUCATION.
    Washington, D.C.: National Education Association
    (Educational Policies Commission), 1951.

Moran, Gabriel, DESIGN FOR RELIGION. New York: Herder
    and Herder 1970.

Moran, Gabriel, RELIGIOUS BODY: Design for a New
    Reformation. New York: Seabury Press, 1974.

Morrow, Robert, Jr. (ed.), VALUES EDUCATION: A RESOURCE
    BOOKLET, Toronto: (Ontario Secondary School
    Teachers' Federation, 60 Mobile Drive, Toronto,
    1975).

MORAL/VALUES CLARIFICATION: A COMPARISON OF DIFFERENT
    THEORETICAL MODELS (Toronto: Ontario: Government
    Bookstore, 880 Bry St., 1975, prepared for the
    University of Education, Ontario).

Mosher, Ralph L., and Sullivan, Paul, "Moral Education:
    A New Initiative for Guidance," FOCUS ON GUIDANCE,
    January, 1974.

O'Fahey, Sheila; Betz, Pamela Cary; Gelsone, Frances;
    Petrich, Ronald W., DECIDING HOW TO LIVE AS
    SOCIETY'S CHILDREN: Individual Needs and
    Institutional Expectation. Terrace Heights, Winona,
    Minnesota: St. Mary's College Press (Plover Books),
    1974.

O'Fahey, Sheila M., "Questions About Values/Moral
    Education," PACE, St. Mary's College Press, 1973.

Ofstad, Harald, "Education vs. Growth in Moral
    Development," THE MONIST, pp. 581-599 (see entry).

Oliver, D.W., and Bane, M.J., "Moral Education: Is
    Reasoning Enough?," pp. 252-271 in MORAL EDUCATION:
    Interdisciplinary Approaches (see entry).

Oliver, Donald W.; Newmann, Fred M.; Bane, Mary Jo,
    Public Issues Series: CASES AND CONTROVERSY.
    American Education Publications, 1967.

Parsons, Talcott, STRUCTURE AND PROCESS IN MODERN
    SOCIETIES. Glencoe: Free Press, 1960.

Peters, Richard S., "A Reply to Kohlberg," KAPPAN,
    June, 1975, p. 678 (see entry).

Peters, Richard S., "Concrete Principles and the
    Rational Passions," pp. 29-55 in MORAL EDUCATION:
    5 Lectures (see entry).

Peters, R.S., ETHICS AND EDUCATION, Allen and Unwin, 1966.

Peters, R.S., "Moral Development and Moral Learning,"
    pp. 541-567, THE MONIST (see entry).

Peters, R.S., THE PHILOSOPHY OF EDUCATION. London:
    Oxford University Press, 1973.

Peters, R.S. (ed.), PSYCHOLOGY AND ETHICAL DEVELOPMENT:
    A Collection of Articles on Psychological Themes.
    London: Allen and Unwin, 1974; Crane-Russak
    Company, 1975.

Peters, R.S., REASON AND COMPASSION. London: Routledge
    and Kegan, 1973.

Peters, R.S., "Rules with Reasons: The Bases of Moral
    Education," NATION, January 31, 1969, pp. 49-52.

Phillips, D.C., and Kelly, Mavis E., "Hierarchical
    Theories of Development in Education and
    Psychology," HARVARD EDUCATIONAL REVIEW XXXXV, #3,
    August, 1975.

Piaget, Jean, PSYCHOLOGY AND EPISTEMOLOGY: Towards a
    Theory of Knowledge. New York: Viking Press, 1972.

Piaget, Jean, THE CHILD'S CONCEPTION OF THE WORLD.
    Translated by Joan and Andrew Tomlinson. The
    International Library of Psychology, Philosophy
    and Scientific Method. London: Routledge, Kegan
    Paul Ltd., 1928.

Piaget, Jean et al, THE MORAL JUDGMENT OF THE CHILD.
    Translated by Marjorie Gabain, New York: The Free
    Press, 1969 (1932, 1948, 1965).

Piaget, Jean, TO UNDERSTAND IS TO INVENT. New York: The
    Viking Press, 1974.

THE PLOVER BOOK SERIES (see individual entries).

Purple, David, and Ryan, Keven, "Moral Education:
    Where Sages Fear to Tread" in KAPPAN, June, 1975,
    pp. 659-666 (see entry).

Ramsey, Ian, MODELS AND MYSTERY. London: Oxford
    University Press, 1964.

Raths, Louis E.,; Harmin, Merril; Simon, Sidney,
    VALUES AND TEACHING. Columbus, Ohio: Charles E.
    Merrill, 1966.

Rawls, John, A THEORY OF JUSTICE. Cambridge: Harvard
    University Press, 1971.

READINGS IN VALUE EDUCATION. Winston Press, 1973 (25
    Groveland Terrace, Minneapolis, Minnesota 55403).

RELIGION AND PUBLIC EDUCATION, A Statement of Views.
    New York: American Jewish Committee, 1969.

Religious Perspectives in American Culture II. RELIGION
      IN AMERICAN LIFE, Princeton University Press, 1966.

REPORT OF THE COMMITTEE ON RELIGIOUS EDUCATION IN THE
      PUBLIC SCHOOLS OF THE PROVINCE OF ONTARIO, Toronto:
      Ontario Department of Education, 1969.

Ryan, Mary P., A Response to "Questions about Values/
      Moral Education," PACE, 1973, p. 5.

Sanders, Nicholas M., and Klafter, Marcia, "The
      Importance and Desired Characteristics of Moral/
      Ethical Education in the Public Schools of the
      U.S.A.: A Systematic Analysis of Recent Documents.
      Philadelphia: Research for Better Schools, Inc.,
      Technical Report #1.

Sasnett, J. Randolph, "Fostering Attitudinal Values in
      Education," EDUCATIONAL FUTURES INTERNATIONAL,
      Presented to the Workshop on Values and Human
      Relationships, San Diego, June 20, 1966.

THE SCHOOL GUIDANCE WORKER, Moral/Values Education, XXXI,
      #2, November/December, 1975.

Schools Council Project, Religious Education in Secondary
      Schools RSE. 72/10, EXPERIMENTAL TEACHING MATERIAL,
      Unit 16, Science and Religion.

Schools Council Working Paper 36, RELIGIOUS EDUCATION IN
      SECONDARY SCHOOLS. London: Evans Brothers Ltd.
      and Methuen Educational Ltd., 1971.

Scriven, Michael, "Cognitive Moral Education," in KAPPAN,
      June, 1975, pp. 689-694 (see entry).

Scriven, Michael, "The Exact Role of Value Judgments in
      Science," in PROGRAM DEVELOPMENT IN EDUCATION,
      Vancouver B.C., University of British Columbia
      Press, 1974.

Selig, Sidney, and Teller, Gerald, "The Moral Development
      of Children in Three Different School Settings,"
      RELIGIOUS EDUCATION LXX, #4, July/August, 1975,
      pp. 406-415.

Selman, Robert, and Kohlberg, Lawrence, PREPARING TEACHER
      PERSONNEL FOR VALUE EDUCATION. Washington, D.C.:
      Educational Research Information Center, 1971.

Shane, Harold G., "The Moral Choices Before Us: Two
      Theologians Comment" (Martin E. Marty and David
      Tracy), KAPPAN, June, 1975, pp. 707-711 (see entry).

Sholl, Doug, "The Contributions of Lawrence Kohlberg to
      Religion and Morality Education," RELIGIOUS
      EDUCATION, September/October, 1971.

Silver, Michael, "Education in Human Values: the

66.   Lasswell Value Framework," in VALUES EDUCATION.
           Edited by Meyer, Burnham and Cholvat, pp. 141-147
           (see entry).

Simon, Sidney B., MEETING YOURSELF HALFWAY. Niles,
     Illinois: Argus Communications, 1974.

Simon, Sidney B., and deSherbinin, Polly, "Values
     Clarification: It Can Start Gently and Grow Deep,"
     KAPPAN, June, 1975, pp. 679-683 (see entry).

Simon, Sidney, "Value-Clarification vs. Indoctrination,"
     SOCIAL EDUCATION XXXV, 1971, p. 902.

Simon, Sidney, B.; Howe, Leland; Kirchenbaum, Howard,
     VALUES CLARIFICATION: A Handbook of Practical
     Strategies for Teachers and Students. New York:
     Hart, 1972.

Singer, Marcus G., "The Teaching of Introductory Ethics,"
     pp. 616-629 in THE MONIST (see entry).

Smith, Robin, "Religion, Values and the Counsellor," THE
     SCHOOL GUIDANCE WORKER XXXI, #2, November/December,
     1975, pp. 4-9.

SOCIAL EDUCATION. A Special Issue on the Cognitive-
     Developmental Approach to Moral Education, April,
     1976.

Smurl, James, RELIGIOUS ETHICS: A Systems Approach.
     Prentice Hall, Inc., 1972.

Stewart, John S., "Clarifying Values Clarification: A
     Critique," KAPPAN, June, 1975, pp. 685-688 (see
     entry).

Stewart, John S., ESSAYS ON VALUES DEVELOPMENT EDUCATION,
     Unpublished monograph, December, 1973. (Available
     from the Values Education Center, Burlington,
     Ontario, Canada.)

Stewart, John S., "The School as a Just Community: A
     Transactional-Development Approach to Moral
     Education," in VALUES EDUCATION. Edited by Meyer,
     Burnham, Cholvat, pp. 149-164 (see entry).

Stewart, John S., TOWARD A THEORY FOR VALUES DEVELOPMENT
     EDUCATION. Unpublished doctoral dissertation,
     Michigan State University, 1974b. (Available
     from University Microfilms Inc., Ann Arbor,
     Michigan).

Stratton, D., "The Development of Values: An Educational
     Objective?," COMMENT ON EDUCATION 4, #2, December,
     1973, pp. 20-22.

Sullivan, Edmund V., and Beck, Clive, "Moral Education in
     a Canadian Setting," KAPPAN, June, 1975, pp.

Sullivan, Edmund V., MORAL EDUCATION: Findings, Issues
    and Questions. New York: Paulist Press, 1975.

Superka, Douglas P., et al, VALUES EDUCATION SOURCEBOOK:
    Conceptual Approaches, Materials Analyses, and an
    Annotated Bibliography. Social Science Education
    Consortium, Boulder, Colorado 80203, 1975.

Swyhart, Barbara Ann, "The Academic Teaching About
    Religion: A Teacher Education Program at San
    Diego State University (In Process), RELIGIOUS
    EDUCATION LXXI, #2, March/April, 1976, pp. 202-216.

Swyhart, Barbara Ann DeMartino, BIOETHICAL DECISION-
    MAKING: Releasing Religion from the Spiritual.
    Philadelphia: Fortress Press, 1975.

Swyhart, Barbara Ann, "Paradigms-of-Reality-in-Process:
    A Methodology for Interdisciplinary Religion-
    Studies," to be published in RELIGIOUS EDUCATION,
    1976.

Swyhart, Barbara Ann, "Public Education Religion-Studies:
    Toward an Operational Process Methodology for
    Science, Religion and Ethics," in THE ACADEMIC
    STUDY OF RELIGION, 1975, and PUBLIC SCHOOLS
    RELIGION-STUDIES, 1975. Compiled by Anne Carr and
    Nicholas Piediscalzi, Scholars Press, 1975.

Turiel, Eliot, "Developmental Processes in the Child's
    Moral Thinking," NEW DIRECTIONS IN DEVELOPMENTAL
    PSYCHOLOGY. Edited by Covington, Mussen and Langer.
    New York: Holt, Rinehart and Winston, 1968.

University of Lancaster Schools Council Project, RELIGIOUS
    EDUCATION IN SECONDARY SCHOOL TEACHING MATERIALS,
    First Draft September, 1973.

RELIGIOUS EDUCATION LXX 2, March/April, 1975. Issue on
    "Values and Education: Pluralism and Public
    Policy."

Values Colloquium IV, THE EDUCATIONAL SITUATION AS A
    MILIEU FOR MATURING, Santa Barbara, California:
    Educational Futures International. Values
    Colloquium IV, sponsored by the Religion in
    Education Foundation, Santa Barbara, May 14-17,
    1950.

Ward, Ted W. and Stewart, John S., ESSAYS ON VALUES
    DEVELOPMENT EDUCATION, unpublished booklet.
    (Available from Values Development Education
    Program, College of Education, 213 Erickson Hall,
    Michigan State University, East Lansing, Michigan.)

Whitehead, Alfred N., THE AIMS OF EDUCATION. New York:
    The MacMillan Company, 1929.

Wilson, John, REASONS AND MORALS, C.U.P., 1961.

Wilson, John, EDUCATION AND THE CONCEPT OF MENTAL HEALTH.
    London: Routledge, 1968.

Wilson, John; Williams, Norman, Kegan Paul; Sugarman,
    Barry, INTRODUCTION TO MORAL EDUCATION. New York:
    Penguin, 1968.

Wilson, John, MORAL EDUCATION AND THE CURRICULUM.
    Oxford: Pergamon Press, 1969.

Wilson, John, PRACTICAL METHODS OF MORAL EDUCATION.
    London: Heinemann, 1972.

Wolterstoff, Nicholas, "Neutrality and Impartiality,"
    in RELIGION AND PUBLIC EDUCATION. Edited by T.
    Sizer (see entry).

Wright, Derek, THE PSYCHOLOGY OF MORAL BEHAVIOR.
    Baltimore: Pelican, 1971.

Appendix

Centers/Resources for Values/Moral Education*

1. THE CALIFORNIA ASSOCIATION OF MORAL EDUCATION. For information write to Dr. Donald Cochrane, School of Education, California State University, Northridge, Northridge, California 91324, including <u>Association Notes and Resources in Moral Education</u> (1975), continued in 1976 by Professor Lisa Kuhmerka, Center for Lifelong Learning, Hunter College, 645 Park Avenue, New York, New York. She will edit <u>Moral Education Forum</u>.

2. THE CENTER FOR THE EXPLORATION OF VALUES AND MEANING (CEVAM), Indianapolis, Indiana, utilizing its own Dendron Press.

3. THE CENTER FOR MORAL DEVELOPMENT, Harvard University. Director: Professor Lawrence Kohlberg.

4. THE NATIONAL HUMANISTIC EDUCATION CENTER, Upper Jay, New York.

5. THE MORAL EDUCATION PROJECT, (NEH, H22372) the College of Steubenville, Steubenville, Ohio. Director: Dr. Robert T. Hall.

6. THE VALUES DEVELOPMENT EDUCATION PROGRAM, The College of Education, Michigan State University.

7. THE VALUES EDUCATION CENTRE, 2468 Glenwood School Drive, Burlington, Ontario, Canada L7R 3S1. Director: John R. Meyer, Ph.D.

8. The "Just Community" Project, Lawrence Kohlberg and Associates, The Center for Moral Education. J.S. Stewart is also developing this approach. See bibliography. Dr. Stewart is Director of Educational Research, Character Education Project, San Antonio, Texas.

9. Research for Better Schools, Inc. Director: Russell A. Hill, 1700 Market St., Philadelphia, Pa. 19103

10. Guidance Associates, 757 Third Avenue, New York, New York 10017. Publishing sound filmstrips of Fenton, Kohlberg and others.

11. "Civic Education School" Movement. Director: Edwin Fenton, Social Studies Curriculum Center, Carnegie Mellon University.

*In addition to those listed in John Meyer's article, "Projects and Prospects: Applied Research in Values Education," and "Where We Are and Where We Might Go in Values Education."

WHERE ARE WE AND WHERE MIGHT WE GO

IN VALUES EDUCATION? *

by

John R. Meyer, Director
Values Education Centre

"Change" and "process" have been dominant
concepts in the scholarly literature of most academic disciplines. No less have educational theory and practice been influenced by these concepts.
The reactions of a major segment of the public are
indicative of a quest to return to the last stable
state. The essays by Debrock, Morgenson, and Tur-
ner have suggested the impact of such change in
values upon various professions. Our work with
parents, teachers, administrators, and trustees is
a constant reminder of Brown's (1971) words:

> "The most primal risk is that one will
> change. And the status quo is comfor-
> table. Security, no matter how false
> or how well sustained by the denial of
> reality, seems preferable to 'what
> might happen'."

Several risks have been taken and changes
made in values education since the last report
(Meyer, 1975). It is again time to capture most
of these changes in a descriptive overview of the
state of the art in applied research. In a second
part, it seems appropriate to comment on some current problems and future prospects.

* This essay first appeared in Reflections on
  Values Education, edited by John R. Meyer
  (Waterloo, Ontario: Wilfrid Laurier University
  Press, 1976).

WHERE ARE WE?

The projects and applied research activities that I am most familiar with are in Canada, Great Britain, and the United States. There is interest in New Zealand and Australia but little formalized into specific projects.

1. Canada

The core of activity has been in Ontario. This is an ongoing effort since at least 1968 when the Mackay report, RELIGIOUS INFORMATION & MORAL DEVELOPMENT, was presented and when the Ontario Institute for Studies in Education initiated a conference and a pilot study in moral education.

During the past twelve months, the following events have occurred:

* publications on various aspects of values education were produced:-

  - Brian Burnham, "Human Values Education: The New Dynamic in Program Development," EDUCATION CANADA (Spring, 1975).

  - John R. Meyer, "Values Education: Some Reflections on a Pilot Project in Southern Ontario," COMMENT ON EDUCATION, 5:4 (April, 1975).

  - MORAL/VALUES CLARIFICATION: A COMPARISON OF DIFFERENT THEORETICAL MODELS (Toronto: Ontario Gov. Bookstore, 880 Bay St., 1975).

  - Special issues of: THE HISTORY AND SOCIAL SCIENCE TEACHER (Fall, 1975); THE SCHOOL GUIDANCE WORKER (Nov./Dec., 1975)

  - VALUES EDUCATION: A RESOURCE BOOKLET (Toronto: Ont. Secondary School Teachers' Federation, 60 Mobile Dr., Toronto, 1975)

* Local educational jurisdictions have either initiated or continued their efforts to develop materials, inservice select staff, and provide consultative services. The London, Halton, Hamilton,

Scarborough, and the York County jurisdictions
have been particularly committed to some or all
of these aspects.

*   The Ministry of Education has promulgated a
guideline for the first six grades or levels of
the elementary panel. THE FORMATIVE YEARS has
many references to education in human values and
one special section. Professor Litke explores
this in some depth in this volume. This has generated considerable interest at the local level.

*   Professional Development for teachers through
workshops and academic programmes has been wide-
spread. Local jurisdictions, faculties and colleges of education, and professional associations
(OSSTF & OPSMTF) have promoted such activities.
In many cases, experienced teacher teams have
been requested from both the Halton-Hamilton project and from OISE. The academic programming has
developed at the undergraduate level at Wilfrid
Laurier University (currently 3 courses) and OISE
and Brock University continue a component in
their M. Ed. programmes. Interest has been expressed in the faculties of education at Ottawa,
Queen's, Western, Windsor, and Lakehead Universities.

*   Preservice programmes for students in training
for the teaching profession have emerged in op-
tional courses at Toronto and Hamilton. Most of
the departments in foundational subjects seem to
offer one or more courses in values education.

*   Annual conventions of professional associations
have included one or more sections on the subject.
The Ontario Education Assoc., the Ontario Assoc.
for Curriculum Development, the Ontario Guidance
Assoc., and the Canadian Education Assoc. have
been a few of those sponsoring sections. Another
invitational conference, featuring McPhail, Meyer,
and Hersh and special workshops conducted by experienced teachers, was sponsored in St. Catha-
rines, Ontario, by several local jurisdictions,
the Ministry of Education, Brock University, and
O.I.S.E. field office.

*   Several publishers in Ontario have taken the
initiative to promote the development and publication of learning materials at both the elementary and the secondary grade levels.

74.

* Local values education projects in the Halton,
Hamilton, London, and Scarborough Boards or jurisdictions have established positions for consultative staff of at least one experienced teacher
who will devote all their energies to assisting
their colleagues in various grades. This is, indeed, remarkable at a time of retrenchment for
educational budgets.

* The joint project involving the neighbouring
jurisdictions of Halton and Hamilton will continue
their efforts in two specific directions: Halton
will disseminate materials at the K-6 levels and
coordinate it with other core curricula, and Hamilton will extend their implementation to include
the elementary and vocational panels on a family
of schools basis. It may result that an experiment will be attempted at one or two schools to
create the "just school". An evaluation phase will
continue and augmented with a student population
of considerable size.

        The goal of the project includes the four
complementary objectives of promoting values
development through the components of:

   (1) AWARENESS to one's own and others values

   (2) SENSITIVITY to the feelings, attitudes and
                   values of others

   (3) MORAL REASONING about value-laden issues

   (4) ETHICAL ACTION which expresses or affirms
                      prosocial behaviours.

        When controversial issues arise either in an
incidental manner or by structuring the curriculum,
the teacher will monitor the environment so that
certain expectations in values development will be
promoted.

        The specific objectives or learner outcomes
that are expected may be grouped under the four
complementary components of the curricular framework:

   AWARENESS - This implies that the learner will
               be able to:
       - Explore and discover a personal value
         system
       - Clarify his/her personal and social values
       - Establish priorities of values

- Observe the actions of self and others
  based on principles or values
- Recognize value-laden issues
- Express feelings openly
- Feel positive about oneself
- Appreciate individuality and diversity
- Identify some sources or influences of
  values
- Identify 6 value categories-concepts and
  one or more themes of each.

SENSITIVITY - This implies that the learner will
              be able to:
- Experience empathy towards the values,
  feelings, needs of others
- Role-play and demonstrate some social
  skills
- Recognize the strengths and weaknesses of
  self and others
- Respond in more mature ways to levels of
  social-perspective-taking
- Express greater degrees of moral recipro-
  city
- Relate personal values to peer and/or
  societal values and value systems
- Demonstrate and receive affection, influence, respect, responsibility, well-being-
  wisdom to and from others.

MORAL REASONING - This implies that the learner
                  will be able to:
- Analyze personal value conflicts
- Reflect on moral judgments and actions
- Interpret value-laden personal and public
  issues
- Use moral reasons and evidence for prin-
  cipled behaviours or actions
- Demonstrate values into a system that is
  reasonably consistent and coherent
- Participate in analysis and problem solving
- Express increasingly more mature and ade-
  quate responses to conflict situations
- Apply decision-making and valuing skills to
  moral problems.

AFFIRMATION - This implies that the learner
              will be able to:
- Express personal and social values in
  actions

76.

- Apply the conclusions of the reasoning
  process
- Test social skills through involvement
  in school, family, or community projects
- Initiate efforts to cope with injustices
  that are resolvable
- Exert influence in a constructive manner
  in conflict situations
- Present evidence that is clear and consistent with universal principles for
  the justification of one's position
- Demonstrate or express the extended
  or suggested activities of one or more
  of the curricular modules.

The evidence from the experiences of the
past few years indicate that these four components
are necessary for a holistic framework. Social
growth and education is multi-facted. It has been
demonstrated that when any one of the components
is isolated and becomes the prime or exclusive focus, then negative reaction and little growth or
development occurs. In social sciences the last
component has been severely neglected and it is
the much of the expression of the other three.
Fred Newman (1975) has made a case for this at the
secondary level when he advocates the goal of "en-
vironmental competencies". Johnson and Ochoa are
wrestling with a social action curriculum at The
Florida State University. The public-at-large
calls for improved citizenship qualities from the
learner clients.

The Ontario Institute for Studies in Education has shifted its emphasis to teacher-edu-
cator awareness and skill development in values or
moral education. A small team has concentrated on
providing workshops and seminars for those engaged
in the training of teachers at the faculties and
colleges of education throughout Ontario. The project will produce a manual or handbook that will be
useful to this sector of professionals.

Pockets of activity do exist in other provinces of Canada but information is limited. Al-
berta is digesting a lengthy evaluative report on
the new social sciences curriculum which contains
a large section on valuing. British Columbia is
concluding a struggle with a rightest group wish-
ing to establish a "values school" that would teach
only Judaeo-Christian values. In Manitoba, one or
two projects are being concluded at the school and
Faculty of Education levels. The Maritime Provinces

are slowly promoting interest by means of an interested core of inserviced teachers. The College
of Cape Breton continues to offer education courses
in values in their summer programme and in confer-
ences.

Few educational jurisdictions have really
placed a priority on developing and implementing
curricular programmes in affective education to
the extent of those aforementioned Ontario Boards.

II.   Great Britain

Since 1967, the Schools Council has commissioned projects in moral education under the
direction of Peter McPhail at Hughes Hall, Cambridge
University. The project for 13-16 year olds devised
curricular methods and teaching materials to help
students adopt a considerate style of life, i.e.,
to adopt patterns of behaviour which take other people's needs, interests, and feelings into account
as well as their own. It was interested in both
attitudinal and behavioural change. The materials
were published in packets by Longman of England and
then in North America by Argus Communications. The
project concluded that adolescents learn much of
their behaviour by social experiment and that behaviour is contagious so that the principal moral
influence on adolescents is the treatment that they
receive from others.

The second project for 8-13 year olds rec-
ognizes that moral education should begin when
children experience their first social encounters.
In a survey, children responded to open-ended
questions regarding their behavioural reactions to
pleasant and unpleasant experiences caused by others.
The results indicate that social learning involves
moral situations and nurturant relationships.
There will be a variety of learning materials forth-
coming.

III.   United States of America

Again due to the many changes and the lack
of specific information, my description of developments in the USA will be cursory. The California
Association for Moral Education continues to provide a forum for a network of state activities. As
usual, there is a continuum from the radical ex-
tremes to the middle, i.e., the value clarifiers
and the cognitive developmentalists.

The Massachusetts' Centers continue their respective dimensions, i.e., the humanists and clarifiers at Massachusetts University and the developmentalists at Harvard and Boston Universities. Much of the work of the latter group is described in the special issue of SOCIAL EDUCATION: Cognitive Developmental Approach to Moral Education, 40:4 (April 1976) guest edited by collaborator Ted Fenton at Carnegie-Mellon University.

In New York State there are two projects worth watching, namely, SEARCH, organized through the Humanities curriculum section at the State Department of Education and Tom Lickona's work at SUNY at Cortland. After several years of anticipation, a major publication has appeared that should certainly give more credibility to the field. Lickona has assembled twenty essays under three divisions: theory, research, and social issues. It would appear that this book, MORAL DEVELOPMENT AND BEHAVIOR, (Holt, Rinehart & Winston, 1976) will be more meaningful for the advanced student and specialist than for the practitioner in pre-university classrooms.

Another development from New York is the publication of MORAL EDUCATION FORUM (Hunter College, 695 Park Avenue, New York, N.Y. 10021) under the general editorship of Lisa Kuhmerker. This commenced in rough form two years ago at Harvard. Now it appears in a polished format with input from a list of well-known associate and contributing editors. This promises to be a very productive vehicle for much of the news that is generated by the field throughout most of the world.

Two projects that are directly related to curriculum development and the production of learning materials are the Religion-Social Studies Curriculum Project from Florida State University and the "Skills for Ethical Action" project from Research for Better Schools, Inc. Rod Allen is completing the 4-6 grade level materials for field testing and Argus Communications will be publishing the 1-3 level materials under the title, LEARNING ABOUT RELIGIONS/SOCIAL STUDIES. The SEA project at RBS is now being field tested at the 7-8 levels. The materials are highly directive and encompass more than 30 lessons. They emphasize personal feelings, ethical sensitivity, and moral reasoning that should promote ethical action. There is concentration on improving communication and decision-making skills.

Another more recent project commissioned
by the National Institute of Education is <u>PLANNING
FOR MORAL/CITIZENSHIP EDUCATION</u>. Research for
Better Schools, Inc., is contracted to develop
planning recommendations for research, development,
and dissemination with the ultimate objective to
develop moral/citizenship educational programs
which will have an impact on American schools and
society consistent with democratic values and principles.

The National Endowment for the Humanities
has granted support for a moral education curriculum development project at the College of Stue-
benville (Ohio) under Robert Hall and John Davis.
Their prior research was published in <u>MORAL ED-
UCATION IN THEORY AND PRACTICE</u> (Buffalo, N.Y.:
Prometheus Books, 1975).

There is also a federally funded project
commencing at the K-12 grade levels in the school
district of Tacoma, Washington.

WHERE MIGHT WE GO?

Though a plethora of studies and publications continues to confront us, there are a number of problematic areas that need a great deal more attention. Frequently one discovers that a hidden agenda or unnamed assumptions underpin certain projects in values education. It would be a real service to this emergent field if all or some of the following issues would be carefully examined.

(A) DEFINITIONS: There is a vast panorama of definitions for a value. There are an equal number of explanations for the interconnections of the affective domain, values, beliefs, morals, decision-making, and most of the components of a larger picture. It may be too early to expect much precision but writers need to be more explicit how they use terminology. Practitioners are easily perplexed by such imprecision and flexibility.

(B) LEARNING THEORY: Developmentalism or structuralism appears to satisfy the desire for an appropriate theoretical basis for values or moral development. However, there are relatively few longitudinal studies that impressively substantiate the positive effects of cognitive development and its impact or transference to prosocial behaviours. The demands for accountability, justification, and "product" tend to prevail in socializing circles. Somehow we need to be able to provide more tangible and hard data to ensure that what interventions are introduced will achieve the expected outcomes. There are specialists working on this problem but what they need is more time and support.

There is an imperative to somehow involve the community more in gaining their support and co-operative efforts. The clamor for a return to the "basics" has the potential of diverting attention away from the concerns for affective education. The awareness of values education as a very powerful vehicle for logical or cognitive growth needs to be voiced strongly. The basics will be greatly enhanced if and when the values education framework is implemented.

(C) MORAL AGENTS: It is even perhaps more important to understand a particular philosophical frame of reference that holds that the human person and the public school are both moral agents. Parents and organized religion are also moral agents, i.e., sources of socializing in morality that effect the learner. It is not always clear who is responsible for what influences. Certainly the parents are primarily responsible but in many instances and for great periods of time they entrust this responsibility to the schools and to teachers. More recently, there are some trends that create conflict between two legitimate moral agents by both thrusting schools into the role of a parent (in loco parentis) and legally preventing disciplinary acts (Berger, 1976).

The assumption is that the school is a moral agent that has the responsibility to promote moral development as well as logical and social perspective taking development. A bigger issue is HOW? this shall be accomplished, i.e., whether by default or by design with preparation, focus, and resourcefulness. One might extend the argument and claim that the school which defaults in values development is a very real partner in the harvest of antisocial behaviours. This is also to say that a person who has not developed a reasonable and functional system of values is a personal and social hazard.

The territory of school responsibility includes the development of shared or unifying values and of personal values which contribute to the fulfillment of the intrinsic worth and dignity of the individual (Meyer, SGW, 1975). If we are truly convinced that movement from heteronomy to autonomy is a desirable and attainable goal, then the "key issue is to bring the facilitation of autonomy from the unconscious, unplanned level to the level of conscious awareness" (Dittman, 1976).

(D) EVALUATION: Another crucial task for ongoing development is that of refined evaluation by means of a variety of sophisticated (valid and reliable) instruments. I have already alluded to the demands of accountability and justification of programme. The analysis of learning materials in values education is refined (Superka, 1976). Kohlberg and team are completing another revision of the moral dilemma and reasoning scoring (see Gibbs, et. al. herein). Burnham (1975), Damon, and Rest (1975, 1976) are refining and completing their studies in moral issues surveys and interviews. Sanders is experimenting with several instruments closely allied to learning materials.

What we still lack is a comprehensive
package that will assess all the major preconditions for morally mature action or behaviour over
the range of school years from K-12. Wed this
type of development to longitudinal studies and
classroom interventions and you have compatible,
credible, and productive marriage.

(E) COLLABORATION AND ADMINISTRATION: One
clear sign of the times in those countries in which
values education is operative is that fiscal re-
straints are forcing a shift in priorities somewhat detrimental to the typical implementation patterns. This is not adverse to the health of the
programme provided one is creative in suggesting
new alternatives for development and implementation. We should not be permitted to "reinvent the
wheel" by duplicating the development of materials or by perpetuating dependence on less effective methods of inservice.

Pressures have been applied to steer a
course of action that demands collaboration and
the discovery of alternatives for ways of doing
things. It is evident that in highly structured
and hierarchical jurisdictions, there must be conviction, commitment, and priority at the top esche-
lon. The support systems will then be guaranteed
for the most vital person, the classroom practitioner, so that teacher commitment will be nourished.
At the school level, the principal must see his/
her role as one of a programme leader and imple-
menter. Progress is made not because it is
"fashionable" or the political thing to do but because human development in values education is what
education is really all about. The notion of
"faddism" or separateness cannot be tolerated.

Sometimes the right mixture of representa-
tion on an advisory committee can provide a mar-
velous buffer unit and a powerful leadership influence. We certainly need to get trustees, parents,
administrators, teachers, and students together
for the beginnings of the just school and just community or society concept.

It is not clear when and how the just school
concept will be effective. It may be a direction
that will prove the most effective prototype or model for extensive impact in an entire school district or jurisdiction. Again that takes time,
tremendous collaboration, considerable inservice
or retraining, concensus of objectives, stability,
and perseverance.

Some ventures in values education are
working with degrees of achievement. More oppor-
tunities are required to provide both development
and implementation. We can rejoice that we have
come this far in the company of so many concerned
and dedicated educators and learners.

REFERENCES

Berger, M.L. "Student Rights and Affective Educa-
        tion: Are They Compatible?" Education
        Leadership 33:6 (March 1976) 460-2.

Brown, G.I. Human Teaching for Human Learning.
        New York: Viking Press, 1971.

Burnham, B. "The Important Consideration Survey:
        A Measure of Moral Reasoning Power." The
        School Guidance Worker 31:2 (Nov./Dec.
        1975) 33-8.

Dittman, J. "Individual Autonomy: The Magnificent
        Obsession." Education Leadership 33:6
        (March 1976) 463-7.

Meyer, J.R. "Projects and Prospects: Applied Re-
        search in Values Education." In J. Meyer,
        B. Burnham, and J. Cholvat (eds.). Values
        Education. Waterloo, Ont.: Wilfrid Laurier
        University Press, 1975.

_____. "Is Values Education Necessary and
        Justified?" The School Guidance Worker
        31:2 (Nov./Dec. 1975) 40-5.

Newmann, F.M. Education for Citizen Action:
        Challenge for Secondary Curriculum. Berke-
        ley, Ca.: McCutchan Pub. Corp., 1975).

Superka, D.P. et al. Values Education Sourcebook.
        Boulder, Colo.: Social Science Education
        Consortium, Inc., 1976).